WITHDRAWN

Advance Praise for *Lead Your Boss*:

"John Baldoni is one of the organizational thinkers that I respect the most. His ideas are practical — and he can help make sure that you have an impact in your organization! Every decision in life is made by the person who has the power to make that decision. If you influence that person you can make a difference! John shows you how in *Lead Your Boss*. [This book] should be required reading for all middle managers!"

> — Marshall Goldsmith, *New York Times* and *Wall Street Journal* #1 best-selling author of *What Got You Here Won't Get You There* and author or editor of 23 other books

"Managing up is one of the most critical challenges facing employees at nearly every level today. In *Lead Your Boss*, John Baldoni's accessible style and uncommon insights bring a fresh perspective to this urgent topic in particular and to management writing at large."

> — Eric Hellweg, Editorial Managing Director, Harvard Business.org

"Baldoni gets to the heart of what it means to lead from the middle in order to make good things happen. By focusing on tactical and practical steps managers can take to effect positive change, *Lead Your Boss* provides guidance for all those frustrated by bosses who are holding their teams back from achieving great results."

> — Eric Harvey, Founder and President of Walk the Talk Co., author of 26 leadership books including the best-sellers *Walk the Talk. . . and Get the Results You Want* and *Leadership Secrets of Santa Claus*

"*Lead Your Boss* explores the power of influence in ways that make developing it and implementing it doable. As an experienced executive coach, Baldoni knows how to make the case for managers advocating for positive change in order to help the organization succeed. And in the process the bosses do well, too. Great insights!"

> — John Bourbeau, CEO, Right Management/Great Lakes Region

"For the last decade organizations have become increasingly flatter, and managers have been given an ever-increasing span of control and responsibility. This means that leadership can no longer be just about the people below you, but must include your boss and perhaps even your boss's boss. *Lead Your Boss* does a terrific job of helping people understand the difficult task of managing upward. Pragmatic tips help provide the tools to get the job done, and real-life stories help provide context for some of the ideas that John Baldoni presents."

> — Jon V. Peters, President, The Institute for Management Studies

Lead Your Boss

Also by John Baldoni

Lead by Example: 50 Ways Great Leaders Inspire Results (2009)
How Great Leaders Get Great Results (2006)
Great Motivation Secrets of Great Leaders (2005)
Great Communication Secrets of Great Leaders (2003)
180 Ways to Walk the Motivation Talk
    (co-author Eric Harvey, 2002)
Personal Leadership: Taking Control of Your Work Life (2001)
180 Ways to Walk the Leadership Talk (2000)

LEAD YOUR BOSS

The Subtle Art of Managing Up

John Baldoni

AMACOM

American Management Association

New York • Atlanta • Brussels • Chicago • Mexico City • San Francisco
Shanghai • Tokyo • Toronto • Washington, D.C.

This publication is designed to provide accurate and authoritative information in regard to the subject matter covered. It is sold with the understanding that the publisher is not engaged in rendering legal, accounting, or other professional service. If legal advice or other expert assistance is required, the services of a competent professional person should be sought.

Library of Congress Cataloging-in-Publication Data

Baldoni, John.
   Lead your boss : the subtle art of managing up / John Baldoni.
      p. cm.
   Includes index.
   ISBN-13: 978-0-8144-1505-4 (hardcover)
   ISBN-10: 0-8144-1505-9 (hardcover)
   1.   Managing your boss. 2.   Teams in the workplace. 3.   Leadership.
I.   Title.
   HF5548.83.B35 2010
   650.1'3—dc22

                                                                    2009015463

Printing number

10 9 8 7 6 5 4 3

To my family

Son Paul, who leads by example.

Daughter Ann, who loves to learn.

Wife Gail Campanella, who makes all of us better.

CONTENTS

ACKNOWLEDGMENTS

∎

The urge to write this book began with the needs of the men and women executives whom I have had the privilege of coaching. Many of them were excelling in their jobs but found it sometimes difficult to get the attention of, interact with, or persuade senior leaders. Their questions prompted me to explore the topic of leading from below, or as we say, "leading up."

The term "leading up" comes from my friend and colleague, Wharton professor, Michael Useem, whose book, *Leading Up, How to Lead Your Boss So You Both Win*, has been a seminal influence on my own leadership perspective. I have recommended it often and will continue to do so.

As with all books, there are many influences. I would like to thank my friends at Right Management/Great Lakes Region including CEO John Bourbeau and President Barbara Allushuski, along with John Heidke, Ph.D., and Sydney Lentz, Ph.D.

My editor, Christina Parisi, deserves my appreciation for recognizing the potential of this book prior to her leaving on maternity leave. [Mother and baby and book are doing fine.] Irene Majuk in publicity and Penny Makras and Ashley Hamilton in promotions all get a big thank you for putting up with my endless queries and helping me navigate my way. My agent, Jeff Herman, is owed thanks for sticking with me and keeping me focused.

Of course, I want to thank my wife and love of my life, Gail Campanella, for putting up with the development and writing of yet another book. Thank you.

Lead Your Boss

PROLOGUE

Leaders are almost by definition people who change
minds.

HOWARD GARDNER, *LEADING MINDS*[1]

Your organization needs a strategic resource allocation plan. With
budgets being squeezed and headcount being trimmed, you need
direction on what projects you should pursue and within what
timeframes. You have discussed this many times with your boss,
but for some reason that you do not understand, she has not acted.

So what do you do?

You take action. You take the lead *for* your boss. You develop
the plan on your own and submit it to her for approval. And if she
approves it, you ask for permission to move it forward. In doing
so, you are filling the leadership void through prompt and decisive
action. You are demonstrating what it takes to lead your boss.

But, as you will discover in this book, "leading your boss" is really a metaphor for leading from the middle. Those who lead from
the middle are those who think big picture and can do what it
takes to get things done so their bosses and their teams succeed.
Very often such individuals lead their bosses, but they may also be
leading their boss's boss as well as their own colleagues and direct
reports. Those who succeed at leading from the middle also are
artful and adept managers; they utilize their management skills to

establish goals, plan projects, organize people, and execute projects on time and on budget.

Not so easy to do, but it is possible when you rethink and reframe what you want to accomplish and how you want to do it. That is, you are not acting for yourself, but you are acting for the good of the organization. This requires initiative, persuasion, influence, and persistence and no small amount of passion. Taken together this is what experts call "leading up."

■ ■ ■

"Leading up requires great courage and determination," writes Michael Useem, a professor at the Wharton School at the University of Pennsylvania and author of an eponymously named book that popularized the concept. "We might fear how our superior will respond, we might doubt our right to lead up, but we all carry a responsibility to do what we can when it will make a difference."[2]

Individuals who lead up are those who demonstrate that they are aware of the bigger picture and are ready, willing, and able to do what needs to be done for the good of the team. Such individuals prove their mettle when times are tough. When leading up from the middle, here are three questions to consider:

1. *What does the leader need?* The boss is responsible for her people as well as getting things done right. As a direct-report, ask yourself, what does the boss need to do her job better? It may require you to think more strategically as well as act more tactically.

2. *What does the team need?* Ideally, the team pulls together; it doesn't always happen because ego gets involved. The boss often then spends time smoothing over bruised egos. However, if a team member were to step forward and help in the "smoothing over," it would free the boss to focus on the big picture.

3. *What can I do to help the leader and the team succeed?* The answer may involve taking on more responsibility to do a job, or it may mean stepping back to let others do theirs. For example, if the team is struggling over direction or resources, you may wish to pass (for the moment) on your personal needs. Give one up for the team so that the leader can push forward.

Turning those questions into a *plan of action* will provide a roadmap for how to lead your boss in ways that make the boss look good, the team succeed, and you emerge as a team player who is adept at making good things happen.

Put Your Plan into Action

Effective planning begins with strong preparation. This is especially true when it comes to leading up. Leading up is a form of managing up, but with a difference. Managing up denotes administrative work; leading up implies initiative. Both are essential to leading your boss effectively. Both practices are focused on helping the leader do his job better. But in leading up, the person leading up demonstrates a degree of selflessness so that the organization can benefit. It gets to the root of what leadership so often focuses on, doing what is right for others, even when it means putting yourself aside.

You need to learn to bring others together to share the vision, mission, and goals. And you need to get them to care about what they do. That's what we call leading others. How do you do this? You communicate through your actions. You channel your understanding of yourself and your mission into actions that are positive and inspirational for others so that they feel focused, engaged, and ready to win.

Your plan must include doing what is necessary to make a positive difference. The difference may be as small as eliminating one meeting a week in order to give people more time to work on their projects. The difference may also be as bold as turning the organization upside down to make it more responsive to internal and external customers. The underlying theme is positive change. That requires a willingness to put yourself forward in order to lead others.

You can draw inspiration for your plan by reading the stories of those who know what it takes to lead up. The book cites a number of individuals whose life stories are excellent examples of leading up. Some stories are those of people who led their bosses, such as Eleanor Roosevelt, Beverly Sills, and Tim Russert. Others are examples of leaders who refuse to take no for answer and lead up to defeat the odds; Barack Obama before he became president is a good case study. Still others are those who rally against convention to effect positive change; Paul Newman and Bono are examples. Another category is those who lead their organizations by merging their values with their aspirations to make good things happen; these include James Stockdale and Bo Schembechler. All of these individuals exhibit leadership and, in doing so, teach us how to lead up to make good things happen.

Senior leaders take note. You should encourage leadership from the middle ranks. Skeptics may think that leadership from below will undermine a CEO's authority. Reality dictates the opposite. When managers in the middle are taking ownership of issues, making decisions, and becoming accountable for results, then senior managers have the freedom to think and act strategically without getting bogged down in tactical matters. Organizations must be filled with people who can think for themselves as well as act with initiative and make good things happen. Such behaviors allow each level of management to engage strategically as well as execute tactically. Developing leaders who can lead from the middle is sound management practice. Not only does it create a stronger organization in the short run, it prepares emerging leaders to be more equipped for senior leadership positions. This practice time and again gives people more room to employ their talents as well as to hone their skills.

How well you lead up is also an indication of your potential to become a senior leader in your organization. Your ability to demonstrate initiative, overcome obstacles, and promote resilience is a critical measure of senior leadership. Furthermore, you will need to influence your boss as well as develop the abilities of those who report to you. Leading up well opens the door to leading the entire organization.

It takes courage to lead from the middle; more and more, such impetus from the middle is what is necessary to make organizations not only agile and nimble but the people within them responsive to customers and responsible for outcomes. Leading from the middle requires the ability to lead those who report to you as well as the ability to lead peers and those to whom you report. Leading up requires all the skills you need to lead a team as well as the application of those skills and others to lead your boss and your colleagues. In truth, leading up is a balancing act, but an act that combines the passion for results with the ability to bring people together around a common cause. This is the nature of leading up . . . that is, leading your boss, your peers, and your team.

> We must have strong minds, ready to accept facts
> as they are.
> **HARRY S TRUMAN**

> A little fact is worth a whole limbo of dreams.
> **RALPH WALDO EMERSON**[3]

The Business Case for Leading Up

In times of economic hardship, as well as in good times, there is a strong case for men and women in the middle to lead their organizations. Very often that leadership will take the form of leading both boss and peers. Here are some data points that underscore this.

First and foremost, there is a lack of trust in senior management. For example, according to a survey conducted by the human resource firm, Watson Wyatt:

- Only 49 percent of employees have "trust and confidence" in their senior managers.
- Just 55 percent said senior leaders behaved "consistently with their companies' core values."
- Only 53 percent believed that senior management made "the right changes to stay competitive."[4]

A survey of more than 800 senior managers by Booz & Company, a consulting firm, conducted in December 2008 as the recession was causing businesses to bleed red ink and consequently shed record numbers of employees, revealed that many companies were "struggling to make the right moves." Some 40 percent of surveyed executives "doubt that their leadership has a credible plan to address the economic crisis." Worse, nearly half of those surveyed (46 percent) lacked faith in their top leaders' ability to execute a recovery plan.[5] This lack of confidence is harmful to an organization's ability to move forward and may challenge managers in the middle to become more proactive.

But CEOs have doubts, too, specifically about finding successors to current managers. And a majority of senior HR executives surveyed agree; they admit that they "struggle to identify, hire and develop mid-level managers." These shortages are growingly acute in technical, utilities, government, healthcare, and telecommunication sectors.[6]

This causes dysfunction. For example, consider the communications issues around why projects fail. Projects fail up to 85 percent of the time when one or more of these factors are in play. These include the following:

- "Fact-free planning," e.g., "no consideration of reality."
- "Absent without leave sponsors," e.g., "sponsor doesn't provide leadership, political clout, time or energy."

- "Skirting," e.g., "people work around the priority-setting process and are not held accountable for doing so."
- "Project chicken," e.g., "team leaders and members don't admit [problems]"[. . .]"but wait for someone else to speak up first."
- "Team failures," e.g., creating "dysfunction" by failure to "support the project" and failure to address their shortcomings.[7]

Clearly, some things are going wrong in the workplace. In good times, you might be able to ride them out. But when times are tough, it may become impossible. So clearly there is a need for people to step forward to correct the problems. And senior management should encourage this. But it does not always happen. According to *Manager's Guide to Rewards*, the behavior of line managers influences "job design, career development, [and] work climate." The *Guide* also notes that managers are responsible for recognition as well as "leadership and job enablement."[8] But, as we have seen, so often senior executives fail to do this. And when this happens, organizations can fail.

Let's be honest: Managers do not set out to fail. Research shows that when managers do fail here are some of the reasons why:

- 80 percent due to "ineffective communication skills and practices."
- 79 percent due to "poor work relationships and interpersonal skills."
- 69 percent due to "person [and/or] job mismatch."
- 61 percent due to failure "to clarify direction/performance expectations."
- 56 percent due to "delegation and empowerment breakdowns."[9]

All of these management failures could be alleviated by good, strong, and forceful leadership. And when it does not come from above, it must come from within the organization itself, chiefly from middle managers. That presents the case for leading up.

Being honest, the case for leading up does not rely solely on statistics. Those will change over time. What really matters is how individuals and teams perform. Collectively, they comprise the performance of the entire organization. Performance is based on leadership, and much of leadership comes from the ground up. This book is devoted to showing how men and women in the middle can exert their leadership prerogatives to help themselves, their bosses, and their organizations to succeed.

PART I

What Does the Leader Need?

KNOWING WHAT THE LEADER NEEDS requires an ability to consider what the organization needs and what role the leader will play in fulfilling that need. The individual who leads up will be one who helps the leader see the big picture, think creatively, and do what is best for the team and the organization.

LEADING UP

The test of any man lies in action.

PINDAR, *ODES* [1]

■

There was little in the circumstances of her early life that would mark her as someone of significance. Although she was born to patrician stock, her mother shunned her, and her father, a self-destructive alcoholic, spent too little time with her. Unlike her mother, she was no beauty and was teased as a kind of ugly duckling, content to be a wallflower at society gatherings. Despite this painful childhood, she became a woman of significant influence, first through her husband and then later on her own. She was a relentless campaigner for the rights of the poor and the dispossessed and later became a strong activist for peace and served as the first U.S. representative to the United Nations. She is Eleanor Roosevelt, and her style of leadership is one that provides clear insight into how to lead through others. [2]

Her marriage to Franklin Roosevelt, a fifth cousin, seemed on the surface a society match. But it was much more. Franklin adored her, more for her intellect than her physical beauty, and his encouragement caused her to come out of her shell and act as what that age may have called a thoroughly modern woman. Prior to their marriage, she did volunteer work on the Lower East Side of Manhattan where she saw firsthand the destructive wrath of poverty on the immigrant classes of the early twentieth century. When she took Franklin to the slums, he was shocked and slowly and gradually over time became aware that poverty exacted a harsh toll on individuals and families. Theirs was a marriage that produced five children and, for much of their married life, was overshadowed by Sara, Franklin's domineering mother. But it was Franklin's betrayal, falling in love with another woman, that caused the break in their marriage. Eleanor offered Franklin his freedom, but Sara said no, knowing it would ruin Franklin's political career. Yet, as her biographer, Doris Kearns Goodwin, has speculated, it was this marital rupture that enabled Eleanor to become her own woman.

Despite their break, the Roosevelts remained true partners, never more so when Eleanor nursed Franklin back to health after he was stricken by polio in 1921. More than nurse, she later became his surrogate on the political trail. Working with Louie Howe, Franklin's PR maven, she took to the stump and became a very accomplished presenter and something of a politician, currying favor for her husband among the political set. She put aside her natural shyness and truly emerged as a thinking woman, but still in service to her husband's ambition.

When Franklin became president in 1933, Eleanor became, as so many have called her, "his legs." He had taught her how to use her position to capture the pulse of an organization by looking behind the scenes. And so she did. Her inspection tours were more akin to something a health inspector might do, looking in nooks and crannies, not for evidence of malfeasance per se, but looking for signs of life and progress. She also wrote a syndicated column, penning it herself six times a week. An amazing feat for anyone, let alone a First Lady. She was the spur that prodded Franklin to the plight of the poor, a commitment that he deepened with his Democratic party affiliation.

But she was more than Franklin's inspector; she stoked his vision of a government that could serve the people. Eleanor also became something of an evangelist on race. It was she who advocated for equal justice for people of color. More important, she urged Franklin to take the bold step of allowing African Americans to enlist in the military and actually perform combat roles, something that had been denied them after the Civil War.

While she was immensely popular, there were many who saw her as a nuisance, a busybody with access to power. This sentiment was especially true when Eleanor, on behalf of the Red Cross, wanted to tour the war zones in the South Pacific. Naval and army commanders were none too pleased; the front was no place for a woman of her station. Yet after she pulled strings to get to the war zones and plunged herself into inspection mode by visiting the wounded troops in makeshift hospitals, the brass did an about face. Watching the uplifting effect that she had on morale made the commanders appreciate her service. She also brought a sense of home to these soldiers, injured and ailing in out of the way places. She was a kind of fairy godmother dispensing comfort and good cheer. Not as someone of high birth, but as a mother of four sons serving on active duty might. Empathetic to the core.

And after Franklin's death, it was she who pushed the United Nations to adopt the Universal Declaration of Human Rights in 1948, a seminal moment in world history. And as she said:

> Where, after all, do universal human rights begin? In small places, close to home — so close and so small that they cannot be seen on any maps of the world. Yet they are the world of the individual person; the neighborhood he lives in; the school or college he attends; the factory, farm, or office where he works . . . Without concerted citizen action to uphold them close to home, we shall look in vain for progress in the larger world.[3]

These are words that any leader, seeking to effect change, can take to heart. That is, to effect change of any kind, it may be necessary to think big but act in small ways to ensure that people experience what you are doing. Certainly that was Eleanor's way, and it worked.

What Eleanor Roosevelt Teaches Us About Leading Up:

- Know your mission, e.g., what you are supposed to do.
- Know how to put energy into your mission.
- Know your subject.

■ ■ ■

Eleanor Roosevelt was born to privilege, and she used it not for power but for influence. Leading up starts with identifying an opportunity, and then acting upon it. Eleanor demonstrated what it means to lead through others, the very essence of what it means to lead up. Additionally, Eleanor possessed something that is critical to leading up: energy. Energy is a matter of drive, the will to make things happen. As such, it is a vital leadership attribute and one that must be cultivated. One who leads up may face varying degrees of opposition and resistance, thus it is necessary to keep oneself not only focused but energized by the task at hand. Energy not only fuels the individual; it sparks the organization, and for that reason those who lead up must use it wisely.

Energize Yourself!

Energy in this form is internal; it is a form of self-motivation. Getting yourself engaged in the work and the people who do the work in order to accomplish the task. Energy is especially important for those seeking to lead their bosses and their peers; it becomes the fuel that leads to the enthusiasm that is so necessary to driving change throughout an organization. To develop energy, you need to know where it comes from and what you can do with it. When working with others, energy becomes an attribute of leadership presence, that is, your earned authority. A leader with energy is someone who others notice and may pay attention to.

KNOW WHERE ENERGY COMES FROM

What about your work excites you? Is it working with others? Is it generating new ideas? Is it providing guidance for the team? Is it problem solving? Is it managing crises? Is it stretching for big goals? Your energy may come from one, two, or all of these things, as well as many others. You need to identify what gets you enthused so that you can tap into it. Failure to do so will bog you down. For example, if you like working on new projects, but you are doing routine administrative work, then you are in the wrong slot. Likewise, if you like working at a steady pace but are jumping from crisis to crisis, you are in the wrong slot. Of course, there will be variations in every job, but if you spend the majority of your time doing what you do not like to do, then you are in the wrong job.

KNOW WHAT YOU CAN DO WITH YOUR ENERGY

Energy powers you; it enables you to do what you have to do. For leaders, energy takes on an aura of its own. Like an aura, it is the shine that appeals to others. It draws people to you. At the same time, people feed on your energy to do their own work. Extroverts, those who derive energy from other people, are continually cycling their energy into projects that involve others. Introverts, those who derive energy from solitary pursuits, need to find ways to project their energy outwardly. For example, successful engineering team leaders (often introverts by nature) generate enthusiasm around the work; their excitement creates energy that feeds the team. They will never be, nor need be, "rah-rah" types, but they are leaders who have found ways to project energy into the work and then onto the team.

KNOW THE LIMITS OF YOUR ENERGY

I read recently about an executive who said that his day was focused on getting up each day and doing as much as he could until he felt that he could do no more. The next day he did the same and everyday thereafter. He was working for a nonprofit, but his schedule was a recipe for organ failure, starting with the brain. No matter how much good intention you have, you need to stop and take a deep breath. Working nonstop day after day without time off breeds narrow thinking and diminishing results. Productivity declines because you cannot sustain the fast pace, and it takes you longer to do the same task. That is, if it used to take you a day to generate a report, without downtime it will take you a day and half and maybe two. Take a cue from Tiger Woods. He works to win major tournaments, but he rarely plays more than two tournaments in a row. He picks his spots to compete at his best. The rest of the time Tiger is practicing his game as well as conducting business, doing endorsements, and supporting his charitable activities. He also takes time off for fun and family. I have witnessed the same patterns in successful executives with whom I have worked; they focus hard at work, but they also engage in the community and their family, as well as insist on downtime.

Think Like a Boss

Energy for the most part is a positive; it is a life force that keeps the leader engaged in the moment as well as in the long term. Work, no matter how satisfying, can become dull after a time. That is why knowing your energy reservoir and how you can replenish it periodically is vital. Keeping yourself and your team going is critical to the mission as well as to the well-being of the organization. It is the force that drives things to completion as well as powers the team up to do it again.

Be Around

So often those in the middle management food chain need to be vigilant to what is happening within their own organization. They need to keep an ear to the ground. To be fair, it is not easy to do. The calendars of middle managers are chock full of meetings, plane rides, dinners, lunches, and even breakfasts. It takes real effort to break the schedule deadlock and meet with front-line folks.

BE SEEN

Managers who "fly the desk" become skilled at maneuvering around roadblocks. However, the trouble is that their vision is more tunnel-like than leader-like. By taking time to walk the halls, eat in the cafeteria, or join employee social gatherings, they pick up the pulse of the organization. Better yet, they are available for people to see and speak to. Employees who know their managers are more likely to share ideas with them.

BE CURIOUS

It is not enough to just mingle; you have to ask people what's going on. Find out what people are working on and how they are doing it. Ask what customers are thinking and how they are reacting to your products and services. Solicit ideas and give feedback. The curious manager is the one who is attuned to her organization.

Persuade Up

Leadership depends upon persuasion. You need to give a reason for people to believe in what you stand for. Politicians do this in public; corporate types do it behind closed doors. What they do is present their ideas, backed by themselves and their organizations, in the hope that people will follow. Politicians get tested every election; corporate types get measured by performance in the capital markets. The challenge for both is to present their ideas in such a compelling way that people not only want to believe, they carry them to fruition. That's how you get results. Effective leaders use all the classic communication techniques to sell their plan. Their playbook is instructive to any strategic communicator.

KNOW WHAT IS HAPPENING

Accuracy is critical when presenting a new idea. If you are a proposing a new product, process, or service, know how it will benefit the company financially (improving the bottom line) as well as performance wise (improving work conditions). Be certain to include the competition in your analysis. Companies, like ideas, do not operate within a vacuum.

PRESENT THE BIG IDEA

Aspiration is essential to leadership. Twentieth-century presidents learned to think big from Theodore Roosevelt — big grin, big words, big stick, big accomplishments. Roosevelt's leadership positioned our nation to take its first steps on the world stage, and we haven't taken a back row seat since. CEOs who want to change must similarly think big and act as if they are big enough to tackle the job. What they say and how they say it does much to frame the right response. Entrepreneurs from Henry Ford to Bill Gates or Sam Walton to Howard Schultz have spun their visions into products that have captured the imagination of huge majorities of consumers and even better captured their patronage.

SELL THE BIG IDEA

It's fashionable to look down your nose at anyone who sells, as if anyone can do it. What sales requires is a belief in an idea and a willingness to bring the idea to life so that others can share in it. Sir Richard Branson is a master salesperson; he has transformed a music label into a business empire. Who would have believed a dyslexic school dropout would one day become one of the world's most successful entrepreneurs with interests in entertainment, travel, and finance? Branson, for one, and that's what matters. He thinks big and sells even bigger and in the process persuades others to come along for the ride.

GET INVOLVED IN THE PLANNING

Those in charge do not do the doing; they supervise the process. While that is very rewarding, it is a distancing of oneself from the action. So get involved. Take an active role in strategic planning. Ask many questions. Visit with customers. Glean their ideas for improvement. Feed it back to the strategy team. And then follow through.

CHANNEL YOUR PASSION

If the leader can find one thing to engage his hunger for action, it may quell his meddling in other people's business. Some leaders pour themselves into charitable works or choose a pet project in which they can become personally involved. Keep in mind that time is a leader's most treasured resource, but if he can find some "dabbling time" in which to indulge a passion for creativity and action, the organization may be the better for it.

LEVERAGE YOUR CUSTOMERS

Your greatest allies may be the people to whom you sell and serve — your customers. If you frame your idea in terms of what they are asking for, you will stand a better chance of being heard. By adopting your customers' point of view, you become their advocate. You champion what you think and hope is good for them. Such an argument applies to internal customers, too.

KEEP PUSHING

Too many good ideas are forfeited the first time someone says no. That is a shame because often the first no is a good indication that you might be onto something good. Find out why the idea was rejected. Perhaps you need to make an adjustment in the idea, add some new element, or combine it with another idea from someone else. You will never know unless you persist in your ideas. If you keep pushing, sooner or later your tenacity will win you some points, as long as you are earnest, courteous, and in keeping with corporate strategies. In other words, your idea might not fly, but your career will. Organizations need leaders who do not buckle at the first obstacle; adversity is a marvelous teacher.

Assert Yourself Diplomatically

Assertiveness may be one of the most talked about topics in leadership style. Managers on the way up want to make certain that they are "assertive enough," while those at the top or near the top are sometimes advised to be "less assertive." Assertiveness by definition is the net outcome of acting like a leader — that is, giving people a reason to believe in your abilities to decide, to act, and to lead others. Assertive leaders are confident as well as decisive; they radiate power and seem in total control. That's the good side. Sometimes too much assertiveness, like too much octane, leads to the "my way or the highway" attitude that instead of bringing people together drives them away.

There is another side of assertiveness, however, that is less talked about. It is for lack of a better term, quiet confidence. It is an attitude that does not proclaim, "Hey, look at me," but rather says, "Hey, look at us." Let's call it reflective assertiveness, or a form of quiet power. It is confidence that emerges from experience, of having endured trials as well as triumphs. It may be a form of resilience, too. Getting knocked down a few times takes the edge off the ego, but getting back up again enhances the ego. Why? Because you know you have what it takes to persevere, to get back into the game and ultimately succeed. Reflective assertive leaders know they can do it because they have done it. Such assertiveness is wise to cultivate and here are some things to consider.

Listen First

A key to effective leadership is listening. Why? Because it signals to others that you value their ideas and their input. Listening in itself is a gift to others. It says to the speaker or the group, "You do matter!" When it comes to assertiveness, you need to know the landscape and the variables. That comes from studying the issues, but most often it comes from listening to others, ones closest to the situation. How you listen matters, too. You focus your attention on others and you ask questions of them to get them to share their input.

Keep It Low

Reflection is the operative word in this form of assertiveness. Absorb what you hear and learn, but also maintain your bearings. Often the strongest person in the room is the one who does not speak. This is true in certain Native American cultures as well as in Scandinavian cultures. People know where the power lies; the one holding authority does not need to advertise it. If you keep that model of quiet power in mind, it will enable you to remain calm when tempers fly and people hurl invectives at you. Your ability to take it calmly often is a sign of strength. When you speak, you do not speak in kind. You keep your emotions in check and your voice calm. Easy to say, but very hard to practice.

Act Decisively

The payoff to reflective assertiveness is decisiveness. Those lacking in assertiveness are so labeled because they fail to act in a timely matter. They suffer from "analysis paralysis" and appear to dither and dally. By acting decisively, you demonstrate strength. For leaders on the quiet side, this is very powerful. It may catch people by surprise. Keep in mind that all situations may not call for swift action. It is often appropriate to ask for time before you make a decision, but if you call for "time out," make certain you keep everyone informed of the decision-making process. Failure to "do" makes people think you are stalling when what you are really doing is weighing the options. Reflective assertive leaders deliberate, but they keep people in the loop as they gather information, consider variables, and respect timelines.

While reflective assertiveness is a virtue, there are times that call for overt assertiveness. For example, when the house is burning, you don't invite opinions on what size hose to use. You grab the biggest hose closest to the faucet and turn on the water fast. In a management setting, assertiveness is vital to crisis management. You want the person in charge to know what the situation is and be in control at all times. Not control of the problem per se, but in control of his emotions as well as in control of people and resources. Returning to the fire analogy, on-scene fire commanders have this kind of assertiveness in spades. They know the dangers of the fire, and they know the best ways to put them out with the men and material available. They are also watchful for flare-ups and blow-backs that can unexpectedly occur and cause damage and inflict injury. Experience is their guide, along with their innate ability to lead others.

Even such commanders as these are quietly confident. They know how to dial up or down their assertiveness. When they issue commands, they do so with authority and conviction. Yet they maintain equilibrium and stay cool while the fire rages and others may be feeling less confident. Reflective assertiveness is an attribute that leaders at every level can cultivate. It may be a form of humility as well as a sign of strength. It brings people together for the right reason and in the process enables the leader to do his job. Such an attribute is especially valuable to managers who lead from the middle because they need to exert their willingness to lead and their ability to do so.[4]

What You Need to Do to Lead Up

The boss needs someone who can think and act and be accountable for results. Those are the cornerstones upon which the leading up process rests. You can think of leading up as a form of managing up, but with a difference. Both practices are focused on helping the leader do his or her job better. But in leading up, the person leading up demonstrates a degree of selflessness so that the organization can benefit. It gets to the root of what leadership so often focuses on, doing what is right for others, even when it means putting yourself aside.

To lead up, you will need to:

- Establish trust by following through on your commitments, e.g., do what you say you will do.
- Connect with others authentically by making yourself available to advise and assist on projects.
- Get out of the spotlight by sharing credit with others.
- Demonstrate an ability to think and act for the boss by demonstrating initiative and the ability to follow through.
- Exert common sense, that is, think before you act and do what is practical as well as tactical to help the organization achieve its goals.

THINKING AND ACTING STRATEGICALLY

It is the chaps, not the charts, that get the job done.
LT. GENERAL WALTER BEDELL SMITH[1]

"We knocked the bastard off" were among the first words that the world at large heard from a lanky, muscular New Zealander, Edmund Hillary, who together with Tenzing Norgay had just scaled the world's tallest mountain, Mount Everest. It was a feat that had killed others and that until Hillary and Norgay's ascent was considered by some medical experts to be impossible. Climbers' lungs would burst and their brains would be rendered functionless, or so physiologists claimed.

Hillary, later Sir Edmund (or Sir Ed or rather just Ed) was selected by Major John Hunt, leader of the British expedition, only after two other climbers failed due to exhaustion just 315 feet from the top. Marks judged Hillary, by trade a beekeeper, to have what it took to scale the peak. And in choosing him, he not only chose the right climber but the right man. Climbing Everest marked the end of an era, or near end, as well as the beginning of a new era. Reaching the top of the world's tallest mountain eliminated one of the last remaining physical feats left to British Empire expeditionaries. After all, from the Empire's perspective, the North and South Poles had been discovered, the great rivers forged and explored. What else was left? Edmund Hillary demonstrated there was much else to do.

Perhaps, it was speculated, standing on top of the mountain and seeing the world below, literally and metaphorically, changed him profoundly. The first change was that he never admitted until his erstwhile Sherpa guide confessed to it, that he was indeed the first person on the summit. Hillary always claimed it that it was a team effort. The other change was lifechanging and more profound. Hillary became a humanitarian. Through Norgay, Hillary came to know the Sherpa people, those who live at the highest altitudes of Nepal and some of whom make their living, still to this day, guiding climbers up the jagged, rocky peaks we call the Himalayas. His love for the Sherpa transformed his life, and he spent many summers of his life helping to erect schools (some 300 in all), airstrips, and medical facilities. This effort also cost him dearly; his first wife, Louise, and daughter, Belinda, were killed in 1975 in a plane crash on a humanitarian mission to Nepal. Looking back, here are some of the things that made Hillary a man to remember.

He knew how to prepare for the inevitable. Hillary climbed his first peak at 14 in his native New Zealand. He loved the altitude and, most of all, the perspective, as well as the ability to test himself against the odds and the elements. He was a rugged sort, and his physique as well as his demeanor suited him well to mountain climbing where grit and strength are necessary, but so too is resilience. He overcame many hardships on the climb but also in his life and met all challenges.

Hillary lived to serve a greater cause. Climbing Everest was a beginning for Hillary. In time he saw his life as one where he could, leveraging his celebrity, which was enormous, to a greater good. Through a trust in his name, Hillary raised money for the Sherpas and devoted his own time and resources to creating a new infrastructure for the people he so admired. Later, he became a champion for environmental causes, in particular speaking out against the degradation of Everest that had occurred in recent times with so many climbers seeking to assault the summit but along the way assaulting the mountain with their trash.

Hillary knew how to have some fun along the way. He did not abandon adventure entirely. He served on teams climbing other high-altitude peaks. In 1960 he led a team searching for the Abominable Snowman. No such luck. Two years earlier, he led an expedition of New Zealanders to the South Pole in an effort to be the first team to cross the frozen continent. His mode of transport — a team of farm tractors built in New Zealand rigged with something akin to tank treads. Some purists called foul (insisting that Hillary use dogs), but Hillary found it great sport, not to mention great fun.

The outpouring of media attention upon his death at the ripe old age of 88 was reassuring that the world had not forgotten him. Nearly fifty-five years after his climb on May 29, 1953, Hillary was remembered not simply as a man who scaled mountains but as a man who devoted his life in the service of others. He was a good man in all that it implies — brave, stalwart, determined, and yet humble. Something of the beekeeper remained in him. To the people of New Zealand, he was a god; to his neighbors and all who met him he was just Ed.[2]

What Edmund Hillary Teaches Us About Leading Up:

- Develop your talents to achieve your dream.
- Work as part of a team to accomplish goals.
- Use your influence to achieve good things for your organization.

■　■　■

In climbing Everest, as well as throughout his life as an adventurer and philanthropist, Edmund Hillary worked the system. He knew how to operate as a member of a team as on Everest, but he also knew how to create a team as in his efforts to improve the infrastructure of Nepal. Hillary also knew when to go outside the system, as he did so often in order to get things done. Working the system begins with prioritization. That is a lesson that anyone seeking to lead up needs to understand and implement.

Strike the Right Balance

One of the most common frustrations I hear from leaders who are asked to lead up is the challenge to think strategically. Often they get this admonition from their boss during an annual performance review. The comment may be valid, but the insight is vague because the boss seldom defines what she means by "strategically." By nature most middle management jobs are tactical in nature. Most managers have been promoted to their positions by virtue of mastering their chosen competency, that is, doing what they do well; they are experts their field. Accountants are promoted into management because they are masters of the balance sheet. Engineers are promoted because they demonstrate an ability to implement a design to specifications. Marketers are promoted because they have developed plans that position their products for success. Such managers have succeeded at being tactical; they have been proficient at mastering the details of their jobs and understanding the competencies of their direct reports who are by and large doing what the manager used to do. Managing a department also requires an ability to do what is necessary to keep the team moving in the right direction. As the team leader, you become the go-to person for getting things done; you do what it takes to make things happen. That is, when a deadline approaches, you pitch in to do the work of your subordinates. You are not micro-managing, you are working alongside them to get the job done.

When you are challenged to be strategic, however, you need to take a step back from tactics, that is, from the "doing" in order to give yourself distance from the task at hand. You must learn to think big picture. That requires the discipline to pull back from an orientation toward tactics and defined objectives in order to consider broad strategies and possibilities. This chapter will explore how you can learn to disengage from moment-to-moment activities in order to lead your team by challenging yourself and them to be creative and innovative.

Then, as you move forward, evaluate your progress. Thinking strategically is one thing; doing it is another, so it is imperative that you develop a system to measure results. If you can develop heuristics that measure progress according to defined metrics, you will demonstrate that you are willing to subject your initiatives and yourself to the discipline of defined objectives. That is, "Did we accomplish our goals?" Thinking and acting strategically are vital to leading up. In the near term, it demonstrates an ability to think big picture and act on that assumption. In the long term, it demonstrates to higher ups that you have what it takes to assume greater levels of responsibility. It begins to affirm that you have what it takes to lead the entire organization.

Rip Up the Box

Learning to think strategically may come in the form of an invitation from your boss to "think outside the box!" Bosses challenge their people to think outside the box because they think they want something new and different, wild and crazy, or at least out of the norm. Truth be told, many leaders really don't want anything different at all. They are reacting to something they may have heard a senior manager say about "breaking the mold," so they scurry about looking for things to break. Sadly, the only things that get broken are employees' spirits. These diligent workers have spent hours, days, and weeks challenging themselves and their colleagues to come up with an alternative approach, only to have it snuffed out by their manager's scornful snort. "That's not what I wanted. What were you thinking?"

Organizations often put people into the very boxes they ask them to break. Organization charts, no matter how lateral and matrixed they may be, put names into little squares and rectangles. Is it any wonder that conformity sets in? There is nothing wrong with conforming to norms — all successful organizations survive this way — but when challenges such as new competition, a new regulation, a changed economic landscape enter the picture, then doing things unconventionally may be called for. Hence, we challenge our people to think outside the box. Provoking people to think more creatively is a cottage industry because organizations realize they must continue to change as our world evolves. And change begins with one person at a time. So here are some ways to encourage creativity that managers leading up strategically can employ.

CREATE REALISTIC EXPECTATIONS

The reason so many employees end up frustrated by their managers who challenge them to be creative is because, as discussed earlier, the manager was disingenuous about his genuine needs. Perhaps not deliberately, but nonetheless very cavalier. So if you want people to think creatively, be specific. For example, if you are an IT manager and you want to improve a process, point your folks in the right direction by giving them metrics, e.g., faster, better, cheaper. When the team returns with their ideas, focus on what they have accomplished first, then provide direction about what you would like them to do next. Being specific will enable them to apply their creativity tactically.

REFRAME THE ISSUE

Edward deBono, the father of lateral thinking, advocates looking at a problem sideways, or adopting an alternate point of view. For example, compare Target to Kmart. Most shoppers to both stores are female; though for years Kmart stocked shelves closest to the door with automotive supplies, things that men wanted. Target, by contrast, is more inviting, not only to women but to all customers. Is it any wonder that Target has thrived while Kmart has struggled? The U.S. Post Office has reinvented itself at the counter. Employees are courteous, helpful, and as prompt and efficient as they can be. The frontline staff know what their customers want. They have adopted the customer's point of view.[3]

Stretch Your Head

When you ask people to engage their creative faculties, you are often asking them to well . . . step off the ledge. So when they come back all splattered and disheveled but beaming with a breakthrough concept, don't leap to conclusions. "Stifle yourself," as Archie Bunker admonished his erstwhile spouse Edith on Norman Lear's seminal 1970s' television show, *All in the Family*. Allow your folks time to explain what they did and why they did it before you intervene. If the idea is not exactly what you wanted, perhaps it contains a kernel of creativity upon which you can build something new and different. Work with your folks. Encourage them to keep trying. Take a cue from the advertising industry. For years its creativity was, and still is, expressed in broadcast or print ads. Now with a proliferation of all kinds of media, this creativity is being unleashed online, in kiosks, as well as face-to-face in "guerrilla marketing" campaigns. Social media is the next great marketing frontier. The outcome remains the same, engaging the customer's interest. How you do it remains the eternal creative challenge.

Unlock Creativity

Creativity does not happen by itself; you must provide a foundation. This is critical for those who lead up. Not too long ago, a good friend of mine, then in his late forties, was exploring new career options. As part of his exploration process, he decided to pursue an MBA. Since it had been two decades plus since he was a student, he needed to accommodate himself again to the rigor of class and homework. Despite the heavy course workload — in addition to work and family commitments — he found going back to school to be "exhilarating."

Another word that cropped up in my conversations with him while he was in school was "discovery." Going back to school challenged him to discover new things, ranging from the quantitative subjects like accounting, statistics, and finance to the qualitative topics like marketing and organizational behavior. The joy he experienced in learning all over again is something that managers would be wise to promote in their own departments.

On one level discovery involves acquisition of knowledge externally and then integrating that knowledge internally and applying it to a specific discipline, be it finance, logistics, marketing, or IT. This kind of discovery never ceases, yet so often it is relegated to training or the classroom where it resides until necessary. On a deeper level, discovery is the process of learning about oneself; this is the journey that my friend getting his MBA was on. As he was learning, he not only gained explicit knowledge, he gained implicit lessons that apply to himself. That where the excitement enters. Managers can leverage that excitement in their organizations in ways that generate creativity. Adopting an exploratory mindset is integral to this process; here are some considerations.

Promote Discovery

The pharmaceutical industry has institutionalized the concept of discovery as it relates to applied science and the development of new drugs and new applications of existing drugs. But discovery need not be confined to the lab. Anyone in the arts, be it dramatic, film, or theatrical, knows that discovery is integral to creativity. Without discovery, specifically putting him- or herself in positions to discover, an artist becomes stale; his or her work is more akin to recycling than renewal. The same applies to managers who do not encourage their people to stretch and try new things.

Invite Outsiders In

One way to stimulate discovery is to invite people from the outside in. The U.S. Army War College invites guest speakers from a variety of different disciplines to speak to its students. Speakers come from defense circles but also civilian sectors. The college wants to challenge assumptions and have students, who are military officers with two decades' experience, think for themselves. This makes for a more enriching program, but it also leads to discovery of new ideas that will make the individual a more strategic thinker as well as a more enlightened officer.

Take Discovery to the Community

Many companies have formal, or informal, outreach programs to area schools. Employees spend time working with students on a variety of subjects, often math, science, or language arts. Students benefit from hands-on attention; employees benefit because they learn how to teach. Employees who participate in such programs find the programs not only rewarding but enriching. Teaching is the highest form of learning; you are sharing what you know with others. It makes you more proficient in your job as well as more competent in working to develop others.

Hold Discovery Day

One of the lessons of Thomas Edison's Menlo Park laboratory was the discussion of ideas, specifically what works and what doesn't. Edison encouraged his people to challenge assumptions; his life is testament to this. Most of his experiments were failures, in a conventional sense, but without those mistakes, miscues, or misperceptions, he would not have been able to bring us the electric light, the motion picture camera, or the phonograph. Managers can encourage such thinking by asking people what they have learned, either on the job, on a project, or from a community activity. Sometimes the manager can bring these ideas to the table at a staff meeting so people can discuss lessons learned.

KEEP IDEAS FLOWING

The highest level of discovery is the personal one. Self-knowledge is essential to leadership. Before you can manage or lead others, you must understand yourself and your capabilities. Buddhism is a faith anchored in self-awareness and discovery. In his book, *Living Kindness*, author Don Altman tells the story of a nineteenth-century Hindu mystic, Ramakrishna, who encountered a man who was frustrated because he had not found God. Ramakrishna led the man into the water and then suddenly plunged his head under water and held it. Just as the man was about to slip into unconsciousness, Ramakrishna raised him and explained that until "his desire for God was as great as his desire for that life-saving breath of air," he would not find what he was seeking.[4] Such moments of discovery open the door to personal epiphanies, moments when you say, "Ah, this is what I have to do." For managers, self-discovery means you must reflect on yourself as a manager and how your actions are enabling others on your team to discover knowledge for themselves.

Organizations depend upon a flow of good ideas. When employees cannot get their ideas heard, it is a two-fold problem that must be addressed by the front-line managers as well as by senior leaders. Failure to listen has cost many a company the opportunity to introduce a new product, service, or process. Such failures have led to loss of market share, revenues, employees, and sometimes loss of companies. It does not have to be that way.

Creativity and innovation should be cultured and nurtured. Bill Joy, former chief technology officer at Sun Microsystems and frequent commentator on technology issues, believes in innovation on a small scale, as peopled by the "number of seats at a table at the local restaurant." By enabling the group to get together informally to eat, discuss, and debate, new ideas may take root. Very importantly, Joy believes that if no "radical" ideas are generated, "the groups should be disbanded without retribution." As Joy writes in *Fortune*, "If you want a culture of innovation, you can't punish people for attempting great things and sometimes failing."[5] That requires patience and understanding from all sides — employees, managers, and senior leaders. It also may require looking outside of your own business, even your own field.

Apply Creativity

There are limitations to creativity. For example, how many of us want a cardiac surgeon to "think outside the chest" while operating on our left ventricle? Or do we really want a nuclear engineer "thinking outside the reactor" when performing a critical maintenance procedure? Or for that matter, do we really want a comptroller "thinking off the balance sheet" when formulating an earnings statement for a company in which we have invested? Of course not!

Truth is, there is room for improvement and creativity in every job we do. Creativity is a human impulse; it springs from our desire to make things better for ourselves and others. Stimulating those ideas is both a matter of art and practicality. You can employ practical techniques to generate thoughts, but how do you manage what comes forth? Most important, encouraging the people who generate them remains an art. Thinking outside the box, anyone?

Creativity is the spark inside that says, "I have a better idea." Like motivation, creativity is internal, but it can be stoked by external circumstances. Many organizations go to great lengths to stimulate creativity. They design work areas where people can come together to chat; they also engineer traffic flow patterns so people pass by one another. While such social engineering is laudable, it is up to management to ensure that ideas are forthcoming.

This does not depend on room design, it depends on the culture. Managers must cultivate an environment where people feel safe in voicing ideas because they feel they are making a contribution. External circumstances are fine, but self-motivated individuals must find it within themselves to generate creativity.

Encourage Imagination

Creativity begins with imagination. Too precious to waste, imagination is not easy to quantify, but it is something that can be encouraged, even nurtured. An inclination toward discovery can foster imagination and here are some things to consider.

EXPLORE THE POSSIBILITIES

Before imagination can be released, it must be respected. Steve Jobs is a visionary who loves to sketch out the possibilities of technology. He used new product introductions as messages to the Apple faithful. Sam Walton was more prosaic, but he spoke to his employees about the new and better ways to deliver to the customers. For both Jobs and Walton, imagination is something that must be nurtured, and its by-products — new products — presented to customers. Managers can take a page from both by making certain that employees know that they are free to think, reflect, and propose new ideas.

START AT THE TOP

Corporate bosses and their successors, from Bill Gates and Steve Ballmer at Microsoft to Andrew Grove and Craig Barrett at Intel, have demonstrated reverence for imagination as they have pushed their companies through waves of transformation. In so doing, bosses signal that the status quo is not cool and that change is necessary. Moreover, they sanction imagination as necessary to business. When employees see that folks at the top of the food chain are pushing for ideas, they feel emboldened to do the same.

ENGAGE IMAGINATION SYSTEMATICALLY

Thomas Edison institutionalized innovation at his Menlo Park laboratory; imagination, backed by experimentation, was *de rigueur* for Edison and his team. A modern-day version of such a lab exists at Ideo, a new products think tank. In such places imagination is harnessed to output in the form of innovation. Creativity, then, is the product. Managers can learn from Edison and Ideo by allowing people to time to think, create, and report on their ideas. Idea sharing among peers, too, is a valuable exercise and can lead to even better and more imaginative approaches to problems and solutions.

THAW THE MIDDLE

The greatest force of resistance to imagination in the organization are those in the middle. Those at the top want to make their mark, so they are willing to push for new ideas. Employees on the front lines are younger and less experienced; they have less at stake and may naturally think of newer and better ways of doing things. It is managers in the middle who have the most to lose. They are responsible for producing results with existing systems. Change means disruption for which they may be held accountable, so they adhere to the status quo, even when it may not be working. Senior managers need to invert this paradigm and hold managers responsible for coming up with new ideas, which often means pushing the latent creativity of newer employees to the forefront.

WATCH THE HANDOFFS

Investigations into the reasons why the United States was unprepared for 9/11 attacks on New York City and Washington revealed that our government national security apparatuses failed to share information appropriately. The FBI did not share information internally from department to department, nor did the CIA, National Security Administration, and Department of Defense share what they knew. Handoffs became fumbles. The reasons why are both political as well as structural. Information is power, so small-minded people hoard it to the detriment of others outside their departments. Well-intentioned employees who want to share it cannot because they do not know with whom to share. Corporations have it easier than governmental agencies; senior managers can mandate information sharing and make certain that structures are in place to make it happen.

Innovate at the Edge

From imagination and creativity comes innovation; all are vital to an organization's strategic direction. Innovation is the engine of free enterprise. The freedom to bring new ideas to life is what draws people from many lands to America. The creative spirit of this country originates with our colonial past. If our ancestors had not thought there was a better way to produce goods and manage themselves, we would all be speaking the King's English. Our quest for freedom — economic, social, and governmental — is what jump-started our nationhood. And our acceptance of new and better ideas from any source is what has enabled us to become and remain the most vibrant.

Innovation cannot occur without creativity. Let's clarify. Innovation is the committed effort to bring new thinking to bear on processes and products; creativity is the human endeavor that propels innovation. As such, creativity is a value employees bring to their work. Encouraging creativity is the responsibility of management, something that people leading up can encourage. Here are some suggested ways to bring it to life.

Challenge Convention

In business nothing stays the same. Your biggest customer could become your toughest competitor. Look at Sun Microsystems versus

Cisco Systems. Cisco bought Sun servers, but now makes its own. You have to be vigilant to the landscape. Managers can encourage their people to be alert to what competitors are doing, what customers are asking, and in turn how they can be more responsive. Make time at meetings for people to challenge assumptions.

Encourage New Thinking

Ideas may be a dime a dozen, but new ideas are not. The challenge is to come up with ideas that reflect new realities, the changing situation. Creativity does not belong to those in marketing or advertising, it is part of the human condition. Why? Because we are seeking always to improve our situation. Managers who live that precept will encourage their people to do likewise.

Find a Place for New Ideas

A good idea without a home is a lost opportunity. Imagine, for instance, that engineers at Phillips had not shown executives at Sony their brand new optical disk for recording data. It was big and bulky, the size of an LP, but the bright minds at Sony saw another application, shrunk it, stamped music tracks on it, and voila — the compact disc. This story has been replicated hundreds of thousands of times, if not millions, in laboratories and product development centers around the globe. The net results are ideas that change our lives.

Produce Hit Singles

While the compact disc might be rated a home run in terms of consumer acceptance, most new products or processes are not. In fact, the attrition rate for new products is over 95 percent, upwards of 98 percent in food products, and about the same in pharmaceuticals. That said, the push for innovation does not mean you have to swing for the fences. Incremental improvements are wholly acceptable. Henry Ford's great gift to the world was not simply mass manufacturing, it was relentless improvement of manufacturing processes. According to historian Douglas Brinkley, Ford improved the manufacturing of the Model T more than he did the Model T itself; hence, he was able to offer the consumer a better product at a better price.[6] This is a lesson that Japanese manufacturers have taken to heart; incremental innovation in both production and product are their way of life.

CELEBRATE CREATIVITY

Pushing back the frontier is hard work and tough going. Often it is frustrating with little return. Here's where management comes in. Take time out to recognize those who are putting forth the ideas. Celebrate the best idea of the month. Make certain everyone is included. Good ideas are as likely to come from front-line folks as they are from middle managers — in fact, more likely from people in the trenches because they are dealing with the issues. If taught to think differently, and rewarded for doing so, they will generate newer and better ways of doing the work.

Innovation has wrought much good in terms of goods, services, and economic health. Not simply in consumer goods like cars, telephones, and computers, but travel, leisure time, and healthcare. Of course, innovation must be tempered with reality. While change is endemic, it is acceptable, in fact, laudable, to hang onto values that matter. And I think that is where innovation ends and creativity rises. We must celebrate personal freedom as well as virtues such as love, honor, and integrity. We cannot innovate away from those human values, but we can create more opportunities for others here at home and abroad to be eligible to enjoy them, too.

Creativity, backed by imagination and innovation, is not confined to market principles; it dovetails with and nurtures the human condition, seeking always better solutions for people and community. You cannot cost-cut your way to happiness and freedom; you make investments in terms of time, energy, and passion. A responsibility, yes, but one that is creative and compelling in its scope and depth! And the more creativity you demonstrate, the more motivated you will become to make things happen for yourself and your organization. That is genuine leadership!

Inspire Hope and Innovation

In the mid-2000s General Electric launched an advertising campaign that promoted innovation. The ad spots were done tongue in cheek. For example, there was a scene in one commercial that showed a jet engine mounted on the Wright Flyer. That campaign worked because it was part of a larger GE strategy, championed by CEO Jeff Immelt, that innovation was critical to survival. Innovation means many things to many people, but there is one aspect that GE hits upon that makes sense. Innovation involves creating something new and applying it to create a better tomorrow. Hope is something that you can build upon if you link it to tangible results. Here are some suggestions.

THINK THE VISION

Innovation comes from forethought. Asking questions about where we are now and where we want to go leads us to develop ideas about ways to become. Within an organizational framework that means you must develop ideas that become offerings, products, or services that you provide. The challenge is two-fold — generating the ideas and then realizing what you imagine. And that's where hope enters the equation. Good ideas flow freely; really great ideas do not. And really, really great ideas that make really, really great offerings require a combination of risk, discipline, and sweat — that is, execution. If you can imbue that journey with a degree of aspiration, it makes the sledding more bearable.

MARKET THE MISSION

Once you've established what you can become — your vision — you move to the next step. Define your mission. But because definitions are dull, you have to proclaim them. You first have to communicate the substance and how it matters to people inside and outside the organization. People inside the company need to know where the enterprise is headed and why. People outside the walls need to feel the passion you feel for what you do. Therefore, you have to do more than talk it, you must sell it. You have to give it some excitement, enthusiasm, and in the process generate a little bit of hope that what you do matters.

ACT ON THE STRATEGIES

Now comes the tough part — turning your dreams into reality. You have to develop strategies and tactics that flow from your mission, but you have to act upon them. Developing the plans can be done sometimes in short order, but fulfilling them can take months and years. Therefore, you have to provide fuel for the process; you have to keep people focused and enthused. You have to stoke creative fires, too. Again, that requires the promise of doing what has never been attempted, or doing something better than it has been done before. That can be daunting and thus necessitates a degree of hope, e.g., a belief that we can achieve what we set out to achieve.

Promote Strategic Idea Gathering

Another way that leaders can lead from the middle and act more strategically is to push the boundaries when it comes to sourcing new ideas. Many years ago I had the opportunity to spend a season following the Grand Prix circuit in Europe. My role was that of cameraman, but more often I was more of a utility person, that is, whatever needed doing, especially when it came to lifting, hauling, or moving things, it was my job. As unglamorous as my job was, I did have the opportunity to observe race teams up close. Back then as now, Ferrari was king of the hill. And while I marveled at the raw power of the highly tuned machines and the synchronized actions of the pit crews, I never thought that what I was observing would become a model, a generation later, for how surgeons manage patient care. One of the challenging tasks that surgeons face is patient "hand-offs," that is, transferring patients from the OR to their rooms.

Simple as it may sound, research shows that such transfers account for a high percentage of patient errors, some of which can be injurious. Why? According to the *Wall Street Journal*, the hand-offs require patient history, proper medication, and a full assortment of equipment, all of which needs to be managed with exquisite timing and forethought. For just this reason, Great Ormand Street Hospital in London has partnered with Ferrari racing to discover how its pit crews managed and planned for routine as well as unexpected events that occur during a race. What the physicians learned contributed to their developing a new standard for patient handoffs that have resulted in a significant reduction in technical and communications errors that could have been harmful to patient health.[7]

Amazing? In one sense, yes. But in a much broader sense, what the good doctors did is what savvy business people have been doing for generations — learning from the best, even when the best is not in your own field. Benchmarking is standard practice in most companies, but often such benchmarking focuses on companies in similar industries. That is, manufacturers study manufacturers; healthcare providers study other healthcare providers. Such studies are useful, but they only end up generating incremental improvements. Sometimes, you need to break out of the benchmark to study something completely different, as the doctors studied Ferrari. Before embarking on such a venture, however, it's good to consider what you hope to gain from such an exploration. Knowledge gained from benchmarking is not reserved for leaders at the top. Those in the middle can use them as checks on what is happening as well as guideposts for where you may wish to push the organization.

As valuable as information and insights gained from outside sources are, it is essential to remain true to your roots. For example, as much as the hospitals can learn from racing teams or lean manufacturers about improving patient care, the lessons in diagnosis, treatment, and therapy will come from fellow medical professionals. It is not likely that Ferrari can teach doctors about cardiac surgery techniques, any more than a doctor can teach a Ferrari technician about minimizing fuel consumption during a race.

Looking outside your own world does have strong benefits in enabling you to do what you do better, but there is another advantage. Looking outside your own four walls is liberating. By getting outside your own place you can observe what others do. It is like being a traveler to a foreign land. Everything looks, feels, tastes, and even acts differently than what you are accustomed to. Your powers of observation are heightened; you pay attention to the slightest details. And in doing so you are exposing yourself to new ideas. What's more, being in new places stimulates the creative juices. You cannot help but wonder, What if we did that in our place? Sometimes the results would be disastrous, but sometimes magic occurs. And that's worth all the observation in the world.[8]

Apply What You Learn Strategically

Good ideas need to be channeled appropriately. In medieval times, scientists sought to turn ordinary metals into gold. A great deal of experimentation went into the process, but alas, nothing worked. Those who embarked on this job were called alchemists. Today we recall them, if at all, with a trace of smugness — how could they be so naïve we wonder with the hindsight of 800 years and the periodic table at our fingertips? Well, today's managers are faced with another kind alchemy — turning information into knowledge.

The gifted writer and psychologist Mihaly Csikszentmihalyi has developed a theory about living the purposeful life. He calls his theory "flow," which he defines as living connectedly with others in ways that add meaning to whatever it is we do.[9] Integral to the concept of flow is communication. Communication is the means by which individuals connect with one another on multiple levels: information, purpose, and community. The challenge for leaders is to use their communication for just those ends. Specifically, managers need to turn information into meaning, that is, knowledge they can use to improve performance. The trouble is that we live in a world where we are bombarded by information 24/7; therefore, keeping up with the stream of information is not only impossible, it is overwhelming. However, the solution is not to seal yourself off from the world like a hermit — rather, accept the information, but in ways that add meaning to what is important.

Once, information may have been power, but today it is more appropriate to say that knowledge is power. Trying to cope with raw information is like standing at the mouth of a sluice gate and wading against the current. You don't get very far. By contrast, processing knowledge is like sipping from a cold water fountain: The knowledge is refreshing, enriching, and sometimes invigorating. So the challenge then becomes how do you, as one who leads from the middle, turn the flood of information into knowledge you can apply strategically? Here are some suggestions.

Create an Internal Alert System

Colonial America created a militia that would gather at a moment's notice to confront British troops. They were called Minute Men. As manager, your duty is not armed response, but it is to keep on top of information. Assign people to monitor the flow of information from senior management. So often in large organizations emails are sent and received, but never read, because there are too many of them to digest. A solution is to divide and conquer. If you divide the task of scanning emails among members of your team, you can digest more of it. Have the monitors summarize key points or report on them at the next staff meeting. Keep summaries simple and rotate people through the job.

Appoint External Intelligence Gatherers

Nokia, the Finnish-based mobile phone maker, is famous for sending its designers to Venice Beach, California, to observe what young people and teens are up to, not simply with mobile phones but also with fashion, music, and design. Immersion in the youth culture gave Nokia designers a feel for contemporary trends that would help in future design and applications. The same applies to managers. You can assign different members of your team to do one or more of the following tasks: observe the competition, watch customer behaviors, listen to the customer service center, and keep up with business media.

Serve as Chief Information Officer

Gather the intelligence people together in staff meetings. Have them share their information. To make the information accessible, challenge your people to present their information creatively. For example, some folks might like to create a skit, others may want to do a wall poster, and still others may want to do an electronic presentation. As the manager, you want to put yourself at the center of it all so you are observing as much as possible. Ask your teammates to help observe, too. Formal reports are not necessary, but active discussions are. Make a whole day of it, and yes, spring for lunch.

Turn Data into Application

You have to be a strong swimmer not to drown in the flow of data, but one way to channel it is to manage it. Voith, the German maker of power plant equipment, requires its engineers to spend time with their customers. By observing how the product is working, Voith engineers have been able to offer product enhancements, among them fish-safe turbines. The ideas your team gathers can be turned into product upgrades as well as process improvements. The application of information to specific uses transforms it into knowledge that matters.[10]

Seek More Information

Information gathering is a 24/7 proposition. Your challenge is to keep the team up to speed by continuing to seek it out and assemble it. You can ask people to switch information-gathering positions, e.g., the person spotting market trends may shift to the customer service center, and vice versa. This not only offers a change of pace, but also a new perspective. Also, make certain you get out of the office. Look for opportunities to attend conferences and seminars. Invite different members of your team to accompany you or attend on your behalf.

When people on the team understand that they can contribute in meaningful ways, they become engaged in the process, and good things can result. "Knowledge is the eye of desire," wrote historian Will Durant, "and can become the pilot of the soul."

Think Counterintuitively

Knowledge does not always lead directly to action; sometimes you will do just the opposite. That can be a strategic move in itself. For example, one day legendary coach Paul "Bear" Bryant, who guided Alabama's football team to national prominence and multiple national championships, was up in the tower, a perch from which he could look down and gain perspective on plays his players would run. He noticed a scuffle that occurred between one of his coaches and players. Bryant rushed down from the tower and made directly for the offending player. The team expected that Bryant, who had a temper when he needed it, would verbally rip the player up one side and down the other. In fact, Bryant did just the opposite: He put his arm around the player, pulled him aside, and complimented him on his "spirit." He also cautioned him to channel that spirit into competition not to his own coaches nor fellow players.[11]

Good football coaches make good studies of how to motivate and lead others. In one sense, they lead from the middle because they report to an athletic director and indirectly to the president of the university; simultaneously, they are responsible for the players and assistant coaches on their teams. The game in which they work is demanding, tough, and physical; it requires a high degree of coordination as well as agility, both physical and mental. With the large size of teams (over a hundred on a college squad), there is tremendous responsibility on the head coach and his assistants to simply manage schemes, positioning, and playmaking. That's why the good coaches learn early, or are born to it, with an innate ability to read players. Bryant knew in this case that to yell and scream at this player would do no good; instead, he opted for a counterintuitive approach — that is, do the opposite of what is expected.

It is important to differentiate counterintuition from inconsistency, a major employee complaint. Inconsistency is a euphemism for mood swings, tantrums, or an inability to evaluate projects, processes, and people objectively. That is not counterintuition; that's poor management, not to mention lousy leadership. Managers must find ways to reach into their employees' heads and hearts to get them to produce their best day after day. Impossible, perhaps, but sometimes the counterintuitive approach works. Here are some suggestions.

THINK AHEAD

Doing something that is unexpected may not seem to be planned, and in the moment it occurs, it may not be. But good leaders are those who know their people well enough to think about ways to keep them engaged. You have to change the routine from time to time. As you plan ahead for the year, determining goals and objectives, think about what you might do if your plan does not work and you are falling behind schedule. Or conversely, what happens if the plan is working so well that you achieve your goals early. What do you do in either instance? Some managers might declare a holiday when the team is behind; others may up the workload when the plan is achieved. What you do depends upon knowing your people and finding ways to keep them focused mentally and emotionally. So planning ahead is a good first step.

CHOOSE YOUR MOMENT CAREFULLY

The evening of November 4, 2008, was the night John McCain lost his dream to become president. Yet speaking to an audience of faithful followers gathered outside an Arizona hotel, McCain spoke of his commitment to the nation and urged everyone to get behind the new president, Barack Obama, one whom McCain said he would be proud to serve. Some in the audience gently booed, but McCain would have none of it. He thanked his followers and reiterated the ideas upon which he had run his campaign. But he made clear his commitment to bipartisanship. Rather than give in to the emotion of the moment and the sentiment of the crowd, McCain demonstrated the true character that has shaped his life.

Don't Depend on It

Counterintuition is not fail-safe. Done incorrectly, you can seem manipulative, as if you are playing mind games. Therefore, doing things differently or unexpectedly must be in character with your leadership style. The reason Bryant and McCain could get away with their counterintuitive moves was because they had established a relationship with their followers. It was based on mutual trust; each knew the other had the other's best interest at heart, even if it took years (as in the case of collegiate players) to discover. Manipulation is about short-term gain; it is typically rooted in self-interest rather than interests of the whole. Effective leadership, by contrast, is about managing for the whole, doing what's best for the team. Sometimes individuals will suffer, yes, but by and large, leaders strive to do what is good and right for everyone.

Hold to Your Values

Of course, counterintuition has its limits. Returning to Bear Bryant, there is another story of a game in which Joe Namath, his star quarterback and later a superstar in the NFL, came off the field during a game, disgusted with his poor performance, and hurled his helmet, only to have it roll to the feet of Bryant. The coach walked over to Namath on the bench and put his arm around him.

As Allen Barra describes it in his book *The Last Coach*, it looked to the world like Bryant was being avuncular and nurturing. Nothing doing! Bryant was squeezing Namath's shoulder hard and saying that if he ever pulled a stunt like that again he would be gone. Star or no star, Bryant would not tolerate prima donnas on his squad.[12]

Still, doing the unexpected when it comes to managing people can be a wonderful way to focus attention on important issues. By employing counterintuition judiciously, you demonstrate an ability to read people as well as connect with their immediate needs. There will be times when the proverbial arm on the shoulder will do more than a raised voice. Likewise, a few well-chosen harsh words directed at a specific behavior can be constructive. Choosing when to do what is a matter of judgment. Even good leaders make mistakes, even repeatedly. But when the good choices outweigh the poor ones, people stick with the team, and the plan and results are good, then you know that you are on the right path, even when you take the fork in the road once in awhile.

Leverage Peer-to-Peer Networks Strategically

While counterintuition may have value to managers in the middle, so too does connecting with colleagues and peers. Some years ago a major industrial company made headlines when it was discovered that it had stockpiled a large amount of a commodity that it no longer needed; the asking price for the surplus had dropped so much that the material was worth much less than the company had paid for it. The stockpiling had occurred for the best of reasons: A junior purchasing agent had instructions to buy it in quantities for a hedged price. Unbeknownst to purchasing, however, was the fact that scientists in R&D were coming up with new technologies that would render usage of the material obsolete. This is a classic example of the left hand not knowing what the right hand is doing. And it was due to single failure: a breakdown in communications.[13]

One way to ensure appropriate knowledge transfer where it matters most is to facilitate peer-to-peer communication. While we all spend much time and energy making certain that senior management gets the message out and lesser amounts of time on checking if people understand it, we spend relatively little time in assessing its credulity. The buzz word in marketing to teens is "street cred," a term borrowed from the land of hip-hop in reference to someone's authenticity — e.g., Is he genuine? Credibility within an organization is best judged by peers. If you want to know what is really going on in an organization, explore the peer groups. Each group has its own system of vetting, a sense of what is authentic and what is unrealistic as well as what is needed. Peers groups foster credibility because they are the loci of information flow. This flow of knowledge is essential to operational efficiency. Without this information sharing, everything would grind to a halt, stuck in suspended animation. Yet as vital as peer-to-peer communications are, organizations do not invest enough time in fostering this kind of communications. Here are some ways to do it strategically.

FOSTER KNOWLEDGE NETWORKS

Encourage functions to meet and mingle. This happens naturally on projects that are cross-disciplinary, but when the project is over, teams disband and resident knowledge is lost. If the networks are preserved, best practices can be shared over and over again through face-to-face as well as virtual communications.

CREATE KNOWLEDGE AMBASSADORS

Supply chain management operates on knowledge, yet time and distance, not to mention the press of daily deadlines, mitigate against the flow of information. If you designate spokespersons — call them knowledge ambassadors — to visit various functions of the supply chain and report on their function's activities, you accelerate knowledge sharing. Furthermore, if the ambassador can take questions and provide input into what another segment of the supply chain is doing, you really grease the skids.

HOLD KNOWLEDGE FAIRS

Many organizations have a tradition of "bring-and-brag" lunches where people from different parts of the organization come together to share ideas. Take this concept one step further. Encourage people to talk up their ideas, but ensure that they meet and mingle. How? Give them a free lunch and maybe even some nominal incentives for showing up. [Hint: Incentives may include tickets to sporting events, movies, or DVD rentals.]

SIMPLIFY E-SOURCES

Knowledge management is the discipline used to manage the flow of information, categorizing it into chunks useful to employees. Too often, though, knowledge management systems become so convoluted they are virtually unusable. This is not a technology problem; rather, it is a management issue. As the foundation of information, data must be structured carefully so it can be retrieved in information patterns employees need. This is management's responsibility. If not done properly, people are awash in data but unable to unlock vital information. Peer-to-peer communications can utilize e-channels such as email, intranet, and web chats to share important information about products, processes, and people. It's really another form of e-networking.

Ensure Credibility

Peer-to-peer communication may be credible, but it can have a downside. It can transform innuendo into rumor, or gossip into slander. The rule in evaluating peer-to-peer communication is the rule that applies to journalists: Trust your sources. And with peers, this is actually easier than in the outside world. Colleagues in any organization quickly realize what's what and who's who. If one person is continually maligning everyone and everything, then his credibility factor turns to zero! By contrast, when a colleague whom you know does good work and is respected, then what she tells you is likely pretty close to the truth.

Still, you need to trust more than a single source. Watch senior management. Read the trade journals. And observe your competition. If there is a difference between what you hear from peers and what you observe from outside sources, you need to investigate and make your own choice.

Peer-to-peer communication is essential for anyone challenged to effect positive change from the middle of the organization. When you can find the information and trust it, then you can lead with a greater sense of confidence. Trusted information gives you a foundation upon which you can think and act strategically. Organizational cultures that foster peer-to-peer communication runs more smoothly. Organizations are more resilient to market swings and more responsive to change. Why? Because the people inside possess what they need to adapt and respond. It's called knowledge![14]

What You Need to Do to Think and Act Strategically

The boss needs someone who can think through what is happening and what is not happening. It's a mindset that leaders can learn to develop in themselves and in others. Taking time to think before acting prevents going down blind alleys. Many preach thinking first, but fewer implement it. Our management culture pushes action first, so it's up to leaders to insist on imagination as a precursor to preparation.

To think and act strategically, you will need to:

- Think critically (and strategically).
- Challenge the status quo.

- Reframe the opportunities.
- Hit singles (the home runs will come).
- Continue to challenge convention.
- Get out of your cubicle.
- Turn information into knowledge.
- Deal with ambiguity.
- Learn to act on what you don't know.
- Find comfort in uncertainty.

PUSHING BACK THE RIGHT WAY

We pay a high price for being intelligent. Wisdom hurts.

EURIPIDES, *ELECTRA*[1]

"What we have here is a failure to communicate." For a time no actor exemplified that statement more than Paul Newman. Uttered by the warden in the movie, *Cool Hand Luke,* that line embodied the push-back-against-authority image that Newman cast not only in the film but also in real life. In reality, Newman was a rebel of sorts, but the type that made things better for others around him.

For more than fifty years, and through more than sixty-five films, Paul Newman moved from actor to movie star to legend and icon, on and off the screen. Successful generations came of age as he passed through character phases from pretty boy star to gangsters and bon-vivants to characters of deadly intent. Newman played all such roles with grace and dignity, working hard to submerge his persona in his character but always remaining who he truly was. His off-screen roles demonstrated genuine leadership character — hard-working, committed, and fun-loving, not to mention very socially minded.

That seriousness was something that extended into all aspects of his life, starting with his acting. He became a film star in the

1950s with the memorable role of Rocky Graziano in *Somebody Up There Likes Me*. He captured the essence of Graziano's boxing prowess as well as his charm. In the 1960s, Newman's career soared with memorable roles in *Cat on a Hot Tin Roof* and *The Hustler*, in which he played a pool shark. Two films in the later 1960s captured the attention of a new generation of fans, notably for their anti-authoritarian, anti-establishment tone. The first role was as the perpetually scheming but determined convict in the eponymously named, *Cool Hand Luke*. In the second film he portrayed real-life outlaw, Butch, in *Butch Cassidy and the Sundance Kid*. It was his first pairing with Robert Redford; the duo would go on to make the very successful con-artist film, *The Sting*. Newman gained his first and only Academy Award for *The Color of Money*, a reprise of his role in *The Hustler*. By his later years, Newman added a kind of gravitas to his "curmudgeonly" or downright dangerous characters, as in films like *Nobody's Fool*, *The Road to Perdition*, and HBO's *Empire Falls*.

Newman had another passion: race-car driving. Newman took to racing almost naturally. He had a natural feel for racing and the skills to make him competitive. Newman won Sports Car Club of America championships and did well on the Trans Am circuit. As a team owner, his Indy Car teams won eight championships with legendary drivers like Mario and Michael Andretti in his cars. Mario Andretti recalls that Newman raced until his final decade, competing in a race at Daytona Beach when he was 81. "Sure you worry but there was no stopping him . . . I found him inspirational."[2]

Of all the ways the world remembered Paul Newman after his death, it was his philanthropy that received strong mention. His five daughters all said that that was the way he should be remembered. But Newman, with his cool blue eyes and handsome good looks, did more than give away money; he created a successful business to give it way, Newman's Own, a line of sauces, dressings, and popcorn of which all profits were given away. Newman kept nothing for himself. The business had started as a lark with friend and writer, A.E. Hotchner, but when the business took off, Newman told Larry King that he decided to get serious and run it as a real business. As of his death, it had generated some $200 million in profits, much of which has gone to fund the Hole in the Wall Gang Camps (named for the gang in Butch Cassidy) for children ill with cancer.[3]

As a film director, as well as entrepreneur, Newman embraced the creed of "creative chaos." That is, as one friend put it, "That was Paul's enduring philosophy, and it worked . . . [I]t was part of Paul saying everybody had a voice."[4] That kind of leadership makes individuals feel like contributors and therefore committed to doing their best work.

Perhaps Pauline Kael put it best in a review written in 1997. "When a role is right for him, he's peerless." Kael wrote that his charm superseded the loutish characters he played. "His likeability is infectious; nobody should ever be asked not to like Paul Newman."[5] Newman was an actor and entrepreneur and throughout his long and rich life demonstrated what it means to lead with dignity and to set the example for those to follow.

What Paul Newman Teaches Us About Leading Up:

- Know your inner compass, e.g., what you wish to achieve.
- Do not let obstacles stand in the way of achieving your goal.
- Seek ways to use your leadership for social benefit.

■ ■ ■

When it comes to pushing back, there may be no better example than Paul Newman, not simply as an actor but also in his life. Newman was one who sought to carve his own path in order to achieve his goals. Noble ambition, certainly, and one from which those leading up can learn. When it comes to leading from the middle, you need to apply both conviction as well as charm, and certainly that is something that Newman displayed throughout his life. Nowhere do you need to balance your conviction more with your charm than when it comes to giving criticism to your boss.

Deal with Criticism

While many in senior leadership positions do acknowledge the virtue of honest criticism, they bristle when that critique comes from those subordinate in rank. The boss's attitude is, "How dare she speak to me like that?" Well, truth be told, the question should be, "How dare she *NOT* speak that way?" Criticism rooted in fact about the business or about the management of that business is necessary.

Since honest feedback is essential to running any organization, it should be cultivated so that employees feel free to critique their higher-ups; and in turn, those higher-ups feel comfortable accepting such feedback. Giving criticism to a boss requires the velvet glove treatment. And here are some suggestions.

BE DIPLOMATIC

If you are going to criticize your boss, you'd better be right as well as diplomatic. For example, if you have a boss who's heavy-handed with subordinates in meetings, cutting them off before they can make their points, it is acceptable to offer constructive criticism. Do not say, "You're being mean." Focus instead on what the boss is doing wrong and how it is affecting the performance of others. You may need to cite specific incidents, e.g., a staff meeting or a project review. For example, you might say to your boss, "I know it was not your intention to be cruel, but your tone of voice seemed harsh. When you raise your voice like that you frighten people rather than gain their attention or their support." Results are what count, and coaching your boss should be used to bring about better results for the boss and the team.

TAKE IT IN STRIDE

Rolling with the punches is not an admission that your critics are right; it is statement that you understand that people will disagree with you. Those in leadership need to listen to their critics, but be strong enough not to retaliate in kind. Leaders have the right, even the duty, to defend themselves, but not to the extent that they discredit their opponents. Edward R. Murrow's investigation of Senator Joseph McCarthy's pursuit of communists in government is one such case study. Murrow, a legendary journalist for CBS News, made the case that McCarthy regularly and ruthlessly made scurrilous accusations against anyone he deemed might be pro-communist. McCarthy's red-baiting investigations ruined many lives needlessly. This story is told with verve and passion in the film written and directed by George Clooney, *Good Night and Good Luck*. In responding to Murrow's charges, McCarthy did not argue the merits of Murrow's investigation. Rather, McCarthy accused Murrow himself of being a communist. Murrow stood by his story and deflected all personal attacks with facts rather than vitriol. Murrow did not crawl into the gutter with McCarthy; he stayed on the high side of the road. Months later, McCarthy self-destructed on national television during the Senate's own hearings into McCarthy's accusations of communist influence in the U.S. Army.

CHILL THEN ACT

When you receive criticism, take a deep breath and thank the person who gave it. Yes, thank him. You may not agree, or you may need to think about it, but you should commend the individual for standing up and speaking his mind. Your reaction will set the tone for what happens next. If you lash out, that will be the last criticism you ever hear. That might assuage your ego, but you may risk running your department or your organization into the ground because you won't have all the facts. If you reflect and then act, you will demonstrate a degree of leadership that engenders respect.

Learn from It

As important as criticism is, there are moments when an employee should hold fire. For example, during times of crisis, such as a failed product launch or the sudden departure of a key executive, it is not advisable to lay on the critiques. Wait for an opportune moment and then deliver. That said, tough times call for tough actions, and leaders need to receive straight talk from their people, even when that talk veers into their own shortcomings.

Sometimes bravery is required to stand and deliver something other than flattery to the boss. It is a myth to think that responsibility lies solely with the person at the top. While the passage of Sarbanes-Oxley reform act makes those at the top criminally liable for corporate misdeeds, it is up to everyone in the organization to share in that role. Such responsibility is not reserved only for avoiding wrongdoing, more often it is about "right-doing," that is, giving your boss the straight story on why a project failed, what can be done to improve a process, or even how to improve team and individual performance.

Leaders need input from everyone on the team. Those who accept criticism are those leaders who not only achieve results they want, they also improve their own prospects for advancement. They position themselves as people who can learn from mistakes and take action. What's more, their behavior over time creates a culture where others up and down the organization feel empowered to offer criticism that is based in fact and intended for improvement rather than denigration.

Find the Right Way to Disagree

Part of leading up means disagreeing with your boss. There is a right way to do it and wrong way. The right way is to act like the professional; the wrong way is to act impulsively. Sometimes things do not go as planned. So what happens when you hit a roadblock with your boss? She will want to go in one direction, but you will want to go in another. The easy solution is to go along with whatever she wants to do. But sometimes that is not always the wisest course. Leading up is a process of doing what is right for the organization (and yourself), even when the odds are against you. The challenge is to do it the right way so you do not end up at permanent odds with your boss. This section will provide you with tactics and insights you can put into action when disagreements arise.

Play it straight. Let the boss open the argument. Allow her to explain her case; she will regardless. Remain calm. Do not try to interrupt. Ask questions that elicit information, but do not seek to interrupt needlessly. Then when the boss is finished, *ask to make your case.* Be organized as well as straight to the point. Invite dialogue. Listen to her objections. Hold firm to your convictions. When you conclude, allow your boss to have the last word. Assure her that you will support her decision. That may be painful, but it will demonstrate that you are willing to go along with the flow. It may also open the door to future discussions and disagreements, some of which you may win.

When you need to let your boss know she is wrong, *check your ego at the door.* Be honest. As her employee, you owe her your best effort. That applies to being straight with the truth, even when the truth may hurt. Easy to say, yes, but here are some ways to broach the subject. Likewise when your boss is upset with you, breathe deeply. Do not push back when your boss is irritated. Keep thinking good thoughts. *Start planning your next move,* that is, how you ease out of the room or out of the situation. And when your boss is venting, steer clear or remain calm. When the mood quiets and the situation blows over, *find time to talk to your boss.* Advise him that he was out line when criticizing you or one of your teammates. Keep the talk focused on behavior, not personality. Be solicitous as well as understanding. For example, "I know you did not mean to be hard on Joe, but you seemed so angry, I think you

came across the wrong way. True enough, Jc
was not intentional. You might want to speak
let him know you value his contributions."

Agree to Disagree

Act professionally. Most of the time, if you and your boss disagree,
she will win the argument because she holds power over you and
your peers. Accepting that fact does not mean you are a pushover.
It is a sign of organizational savvy. It also opens the door for further dialogue. Make it clear that while you disagree behind closed
doors, you will not embarrass your boss in a meeting with higher-
ups. You will demonstrate your support. That gives the boss the security to know that you have her back. There will be times to voice
your opposition, but you don't want to do so in ways that will
make your boss look foolish.

Never acquiesce in matters of conscience or ethics. If your boss
asks you to do something illegal, a flat no is the only acceptable answer. This is very easy to say but can be hard to implement if you
fear losing your job. However, losing your job may be preferable to
a jail sentence. There are many people serving prison time for
going along with a supervisor's scheme. Stand up for what is right.
That is the ultimate measure of leading up.

Bosses are owed open and honest feedback just as employees
are. A coaching conversation opens the door for genuine dialogue.
Position yourself as the big-picture thinker, that is, providing insight that the boss can apply to his situation. Frame your conversation in ways that demonstrate that you are interested more in
what's good for the team than what is good for yourself.

Demand Relevancy

The other day a friend of mine said that he was ready to implement a piece of advice I had given him years ago and had repeated

course of our conversation. There was nothing remarkable
my advice. What was interesting was his reaction. He said,
"You've been telling me to do this for years, but now it makes
sense." That's a lesson that is applicable to every leader. So much of
how leaders communicate depends upon imparting the right message at the right time. If the person is not interested or does not see
any value in the message, then the message is nothing more than
words. In one ear and out the other! Therefore, leaders who are
concerned with what they say — and what leader isn't — need to
ask themselves: Is this relevant?

Never assume that people understand you unless you have
taken the time to explain things. And if you want people to do
things the right way, you have to teach them; you must make lessons about business relevant to their work. Furthermore, you have
to prepare people to receive the message. As CEO of General Electric, Jack Welch shepherded three organizational transformations.
In the process he became adept at delivering his message multiple
times because he understood that everyone is not ready to understand it simultaneously. For some in the audience, the message
was something they could implement; for others the message was
irrelevant. Welch had the good sense to stay on message so that he
could reach people when they were the most receptive.[6]

Relevancy is vital to leading from the middle. Without it, what
you ask people to do is by extension irrelevant. And if it is irrelevant, they will not do it. So when a leader has something important to say, she must determine relevancy as well as readiness. Here
are three questions you can ask to make that determination.

WHAT'S GOING ON?

So often managers open their mouths before looking to see who's
listening and what's happening. For example, a corporate directive
will cascade down through layers of management asking that all
managers convene their people and give the marching orders.
Nothing wrong with cascades, but what is overlooked is that the
people in the room may be so overloaded that to take time out for

yet another meeting takes them away from their work. So rather than determining ways to dispense the communication, the manager does what he's told. Is it any wonder that messages fall on deaf ears? Better to take the temperature of the department and find the right time to dispense the message. Or better yet dispense in small doses to smaller groups of people. Yes, this may be more work for the manager, but it certainly ensures that the manager connects with his people.

What Do People Need to Know Now?

We live in an era of information overload. Information for its own sake is irrelevant, yet every day we are bombarded by messages from our management who do not consider the context. What is relevant is knowledge. Knowledge is information you apply to your situation or your problem. One manufacturing organization prided itself on communication; it used communication to drive its change initiative. Yet when it asked people about the communications, people responded that they felt overwhelmed. Employees wanted to be in the loop, but not strangled by it. So this enterprise pared the information flow by asking, What do people need to know to do their jobs?[7] The answers will be different according to where you work; finance people need information about investments; marketing people need information about sales trends; and manufacturers need order tallies. Each discipline will turn information into knowledge that it can apply to jobs.

What Can I Do to Make the Message Real?

This question gets to the nub of leadership, investment of self into others. For some managers, relevancy emerges from coaching, either from setting expectations, gaining agreement, or providing feedback. For other managers, relevancy develops from the manager's actually working the project with her people. You want to be careful not to micromanage so that you take out all decision making, but you want to use your participation to further the project as well as teach others how to do their jobs. And what's more, managerial participation demonstrates solidarity with employees and further promotes trust. It makes people say, I can count on that person.

Create Relevancy Through Action

Relevancy may not wait for the right moment. It is often up to the leader to make the message relevant, to add the impetus to the message to give it momentum. For example, if a newly launched product has just hit the market and suddenly develops a performance flaw, then what becomes more pertinent is action. You want to ask questions to determine the scope of the problem as well as questions to determine how you can apply your resources, but what may be most important is immediate action. The project manager then makes his message very timely by calling everyone together and issuing a call to action, followed by a means to put the call into action.

Making communications relevant is essential to successful leadership. Managers who issue directives without considering what's going on around them do so at their own peril. It is a key reason why so many messages are nothing more than hot air, which, contrary to their overheated puffery, leave people cold. Communications fail precisely because they are not relevant to an employee's work life. By contrast, communications that succeed are those that touch a nerve, excite a passion, and engage the employee's heart and mind in ways that encourage a response. That is relevancy at its highest degree, and it opens the door to genuine understanding between leader and follower where possibilities become actions.

Accept Criticism

One of the most shameful things to emerge from the credit crisis that so adversely affected the financial services industry was the lack of leadership. Many senior executives realized that serious problems were developing, yet few stepped forward to address the situation. Not until the investment banker Lehman Brothers went bankrupt in September 2008 did the severity of the crisis come to light in a public sense, and by then it was too late to use conventional means to restore confidence in the credit markets. It required the intervention of government funding in the form of the Troubled Asset Relief Program (TARP) to provide a measure of liquidity and stability to the financial sector. Run and hide is not an option when faced with bad news. Better to confront your adversaries and deal with them in the open than play games.

It takes courage, and it is not without risk, to face your adversaries in public, in particular, when you may have made a misstep. Professional athletes sometimes moan and groan that they are unfairly criticized because their miscues are made in public. None of the rest of us, they protest, are subjected to such scrutiny. True, but few of us are making the mega millions that these athletes do. The same applies to large organizations. Their top folks are making big bucks, and their companies are public. Transparency rules, especially during times of hardship and crisis. People demand answers to big questions; they seek answers to why things are not going well. So when adversity threatens you, stand tall and listen. Here are two suggestions.

OWN UP TO THE PROBLEM

When a company experiences problems with products or services, it needs to acknowledge them. One solution is to hold focus groups with customers as a means of creating dialogue. Engaging customers via social media tools such as blogs, messaging, and wikis is another step. The challenge is to allow for the exchange of ideas. Conversation is much better than confrontation. Ideas and solutions may come from open discussion. How you as a middle manager engage your critics is important. Never speak down to them; treat them as you would a stakeholder. Why? Because they are stakeholders in the court of public perception. Their opinions matter. The good news is that when you win over a critic, you often create an advocate.

Make Things Right

In the 1990s Nike found its stylish image dissolving in the hot water of public opinion over its use of substandard and low wage factories in Asia. Nike owned up to the issue and improved wage, safety, and environmental standards of its supplier factories. It led the way for other shoe manufacturers. Clever PR is not enough; you need to make real change, too.

Learn from Criticism

Confronting critics in public has merit, but there are times when it is inappropriate — chiefly, in personnel issues. For example, the public does not need to know about reasons for firing employees over personal discretions or ethical lapses. It is enough to terminate the individual and move forward. At the same time, all criticism is not equal. Some may come from disgruntled customers with an unfounded grievance; they may be chronic complainers. However, putting them down in public is not the answer; if you treat them with respect, you deflate the very ground upon which they rail against you.

All large companies have their faults; every one of them, like every one of us, can do better. Companies that own up to problems understand that there is more to be gained from talking with critics than stonewalling them. Confronting critics is never fun, never enjoyed, but it is necessary. If you approach the process with a sense of dignity, you will learn, and ultimately your organization will prevail. If not, and you attempt to run and hide, you may fade into oblivion, along with your enterprise. The choice is yours.

Avoid the Zero Sum Game

In the dark days of the Iraqi war and occupation, a U.S. State Department official lamented the Iraqis' inability to negotiate with each other as well as with occupying forces. One of the difficulties the diplomat noted was that the Iraqis under Saddam Hussein did not negotiate; all governmental transactions were "winner take all" propositions.[8] One of the temptations of people who vie for authority and power is the desire to hoard all the winnings for themselves. Striving for it undercuts any need to negotiate, and as a result only one side wins. We call this effort a "zero sum game."

Zero sum games occur with regularity within the corporate environment. Zero sum games in the corporate world arise when people with power impose it without taking into consideration larger implications. The challenge of people in power, therefore, is to learn to share it, not simply because it may be the right thing to do, but because it is the most effective way to lead and to manage others. This is genuine negotiation, and it is rooted in open and honest communications.

One side ends up dominating, obliterating the culture of the other. Organizations have life cycles, just as people and products do, so change is not a bad thing. What can be harmful is when the stronger party believes it is better in every way, including people and processes. That robs the new organization of the rich gene pool of talent of the acquired side. Yet it happens.

While most middle managers will not be acquiring companies, they will be recruiting, hiring, and retaining talent throughout their careers. In fact, such people management is critical to success. Therefore, when it comes to people, managers must learn to incorporate rather than dominate, to welcome rather than repel, and to enrich rather than exile. Put another way, managers in the middle must negotiate strategies that avoid the zero sum game in favor of the win-win proposition. This way you build trust of those above you and below you. Here are some ways to make this happen.

MAKE A HABIT OF YES

Dictators rule by telling everyone else but themselves no. If you invert that equation and say yes to ideas, you signal three things: One, you want advice; two, you cannot do it alone; and three, you believe in teamwork. Saying yes more than no does not make a manager wishy-washy or soft; it connotes her as one who understands that management is the art of getting things done the *right* way and with the *right* people. Saying yes more often also generates more goodwill, which in turn helps build greater levels of trust. And when employees trust their manager, they will be more ready to accept the nos that are part of any management endeavor.

INVOLVE OTHERS

Negotiation is a two-way street. If the person at the top of the food chain makes all the decisions, you have no negotiation, you have a dictatorship supported by subservience. Leaders who want to get things done know that their chances of success improve exponentially when they involve others in the identification of issues, the diagnosis of problems, and the formulation of solutions. One successful entrepreneur in the home service business practices "servant leadership"; he considers it his job to serve franchise and employee needs, working carefully to structure win-win propositions for all interested parties. There is an added benefit. Such involvement breeds creativity; people think more and better when they feel someone actually listens to them.

DEFER TO THE JUDGMENT OF OTHERS

When decisions can be made by others, push for it. For example, if an operations person offers a plan for streamlining a process or even eliminating it, listen carefully. Such individuals are closest to the action, so they may often have the best information by which to form a decision and make it. One former retail executive I know made a practice of touring company stores soliciting ideas from store managers before dictating orders from headquarters. Managers who ask for the input of those on the front lines are managers who are most in tune with the reality of the situation and therefore can trust their people to make the right choices.

BE MAGNANIMOUS

One of the most tenacious leaders in history was Winston Churchill. When he happened upon an idea that he liked, he clung to it, regardless of the odds. Yet when victory was his, he was generous to the vanquished. He did not lord over them; he sought them as future allies. Managers who are magnanimous endear people to them, and that is essential in an organization when success is less about winning and losing and more about getting along and getting things done.

Decide to Decide

Too much negotiation, however, leads to analysis paralysis. Should I or shouldn't I may be okay for Hamlet, but not for middle managers. Contemplation is essential, as is taking input from others, but somehow, some way, managers must decide. That is the manager's responsibility and how she exerts leadership. For example, when a project comes to the fork in the road, it is up to the project manager to make the call. Solicit input from affected parties but make the decision. The only thing worse than making the wrong decision may be not making a decision at all. You can learn from a mistake, but you cannot learn much from standing too long at the fork in the road. Besides, you just might get run over by people and organizations who are more clever as well as more swift.

What is essential to avoiding the zero sum game is creating opportunities for people to maintain a sense of autonomy as well as pride. Triumphing over an opponent might be appropriate for the boxing ring, but it is not good form within an organization. Too often managers who seek to win at all costs forget that they cannot do it themselves; they will need the ideas and support of everyone on the team. Business may be a game for winners and losers, but management is a plus-plus proposition that can only work when people can cooperate and collaborate. That's the secret to getting things done!

Get Down to It

Managers who lead from the middle can use the journey of discovery as a means of challenging their employees to think for themselves and, very importantly, to do for themselves. Discovery is really a process of liberation. When discovery works, it's like throwing on the light switch; things become visible. Obstacles that once seemed impenetrable dissolve with the illumination of thought. For example, take a new process implementation challenge. Often the technology is sound; it's the application that fails outside of the lab. Instead of trying to solve it, turn it over to the team to find a solution. Likely they will. The same may hold for a new product introduction. Engage the sales team with customers to make for a smooth launch that coordinates marketing, distribution, delivery, and sales as one process.

We look back at the fifteenth, sixteenth, and seventeeth centuries as the Age of Discovery. Today the twenty-first century cries out for men and women who possess a similar spirit of wanting to explore different branches of knowledge as a means of bringing more expertise to their jobs as well as more understanding of themselves and their own capabilities. All it takes is a manager who is willing to discover with them. An exhilarating prospect!

Act on What You Don't Know

Sometime in the early 1930s, a young Army colonel was assigned a plum post: to lead officer training at Fort Benning, Georgia. Fort Benning in those days was where officers punched their ticket on the way up (up being a relative term since promotions were hard to come by in this particular age). Benning was more finishing school than military training; emphasis was placed on drill and recitation. This colonel knew better; as a staff aide to General "Blackjack" Pershing in the First World War, he saw first-hand what happens when commanders lose focus in what we now call the "fog of war." Repetition and elocution would not do for the future officers, so the colonel revamped the curriculum, placing emphasis on battle maneuvers and tactics. He created exercises that simulated combat so that officers would get a taste of what it was like to make decisions not only under pressure, but with little or no concrete information. This form of training played a pivotal role in preparing those who would one day lead U.S. troops into a future conflict then looming on the horizon — World War II. The colonel was George C. Marshall and what he accomplished in business terms was teach his charges to deal with ambiguity.[9]

Ambiguity is not a topic that is discussed much in many MBA programs. The emphasis in managerial education, and not without merit, is on research, analysis, and decision making. Quantitative skills are prized; after all, businesses mark progress according to predefined metrics related to development, operations, logistics, and revenues. However, the real world, as any savvy businessperson will tell you, is not reduced to columns of numbers. Ambiguity is more the rule of the day, and in fact, many leadership development programs teach and later evaluate their leaders on their ability to deal with uncertainty. Change is a constant in management, and for that reason the unknowns often outweigh the certainties, especially for those in middle management who are being pushed by forces from below as well as pulled from powers from above.

Dealing with ambiguity may be more art than science. Analysis is paramount, but the analysis is often of people and situations rather than hard-core data. As a middle manager, learning to manage in an ambiguous environment is essential to rising to the top, but it is also vital to the successful running of the enterprise. Your senior leadership is counting on you to demonstrate clarity. Leading in ambiguity is a balancing act; it requires attentiveness to people who report to you as well as those to whom you report.

READ THE SITUATION

What's going on? That's a question managers should ask themselves regularly. The answers to that question will reveal what is happening as well as what is not happening. For example, if a team is pushing to meet a deadline, this question will provide a status update (what's happening), but if the manager pushes below the surface, she may discover that the team is moving forward, but it may not have the necessary manpower to meet the deadline (what's not happening). It will then be up to the manager to reconcile this ambiguity between surface calm and disaster on the horizon. Good managers know how to handle the situation by pulling people onto the project or even pitching in themselves. The proper read resolves ambiguity for the moment.

READ THE PEOPLE

Knowing what people want is essential to leading them. The easiest way to determine need is to observe how people work and how they interact. Reading people is more than surface scanning; it involves reflection on performance combined with a look at what people have accomplished and what they are capable of accomplishing. Decisions about whom to promote depend upon accurate reading of people. But, so too do decisions about team assignments and job rotations.

KNOW THE OPPOSITION

When George Patton put his Third Army into France after D-Day, he made a mad dash toward the German border, much to the chagrin of General Eisenhower and the horror of Field Marshall Montgomery. How could he be so rash? his critics railed. On the contrary, Patton knew his adversary, chiefly General Irwin Rommel, and knew that if he applied a blitzkrieg-like strategy toward the Wehrmacht already reeling from defeat in Normandy, he could make it to Germany. Sadly, he was pulled back, a factor that some historians think may have prolonged the war an additional six months.[10]

On a more civil front, Coca Cola knows PepsiCo and vice versa; each can predict what the other will do when it comes to fighting for shelf space, vending, and fountain. As a result, both can plan ahead.

Where uncertainty comes into play is in the relatively new competitive landscapes that include flavored drinks and bottled waters. Since such markets are relatively new, and consumers more fickle, each tries to outdo the other in terms of discounts, coupons, and promotions. Certainty, therefore, prevails in stable markets, e.g., soda, but not in emerging markets, e.g., vitamin waters and energy drinks. It is vital to know in which market you are competing.

ACT DECISIVELY

Decisiveness is a leadership hallmark; making a decision is the leader's prerogative. Take the situation of a senior VP who must decide whether to commit research dollars to a new project or hold back to see how the market develops. Research and analysis will provide clues to the ultimate answer, but it will be up to the leader to pull the trigger on the deal. Deciding to push ahead or hang back is clear cut, but either course will have consequences. The new product may create a new opportunity, or it may not. Holding back may be a safe choice, but it could cost the company millions in lost opportunity. But making the decision is imperative. [When in doubt, remember this adage: Not to decide is to decide. That will give you the heart to act.]

REVISIT THE SITUATION

Change is a force that creates ambiguity, so after you've decided and acted, you need to check in with the consequences of your decision. For example, if you have decided to launch a process improvement, and after six months, things are stalled, you need to find out why. It may be part of the change process, or it may be because people do not understand what they are supposed to do or lack resources to do anything about it. As the leader, it is your opportunity to read the situation and the people involved and decide again, perhaps to stay the course or to provide additional resources. Taking the time to revisit the situation demonstrates that ambiguity is not hindering you; you are managing it.

TUNE INTO THE SILENCE

Political pundit and author, Chris Matthews, writes in *Hardball* that the late Tip O'Neill, Speaker of the House and Matthews' one-time boss, always began his working day with the same question, "Whaddaya hear?" O'Neill had a voracious appetite for information about what members of the House, their constituents, and the White House were saying and doing. O'Neill was also savvy enough to know what he didn't know and so he would listen to the silence.[11] Managers can learn from the old Boston pol by listening to what people do not say as well as how they say it. For example, if an employee is saying that everything's fine, but will not make eye contact, perhaps he is not telling the truth, not to be deceitful but because he is fearful of the consequences. Likewise, if things really are quiet, that is, no chatter in the hallway, cafeteria, and break rooms, something is definitely wrong. Too much silence can be deadly.

ACT AS BEST YOU CAN

No manager wants to make decisions in a vacuum, nor should he, but few managers will have the luxury of making decisions as one would play chess — with all the variables laid out in neat squares. What happens off the board, e.g., in the real world, may tilt the entire board, spilling all of the pawns, knights, bishops, plus king and queen, onto the floor. That is what happens when a new competitor enters the picture, the economy takes a dive, or your chief product suddenly fails. Business is about addressing uncertainty and, more important, finding ways to cope and eventually succeed despite the odds. Within this environment of uncertainty, you must decide and live with the consequences. Not deciding only prolongs the uncertainty.

EMBRACE AMBIGUITY

"It is the pull of opposite poles that stretches souls," wrote Eric Hoffer. "And only stretched souls make music." This is a theme that Jan Carlzon implemented when he led SAS airlines. Management wants to control; creatives want to innovate. It is the leader's responsibility to nurture the tension. Managers who lead up need to find a way to keep the analytical side of the business humming, as well as the innovation side flowing, so that there is a balance between control and creativity. Such a balance may tilt more to the control side, but it can never be allowed to thwart the creative side, otherwise the business will die from lack of original thinking.[12]

Leave No Room for Ambiguity

Ambiguity may be a norm in management, but there are instances in which there can be no ambiguity, most especially in cases of ethics. Shades of gray around ethical issues are what lead people and organizations to a slackening of standards. For example, if a manager knows that his boss "fudges" his expense account, he may feel "entitled" to do the same. Pretty soon, other numbers are similarly inflated or deflated or expensed or not expensed. Petty larceny may lead to graver crimes such as embezzlement. Lack of clarity, that is, ambiguity, makes such behavior seemingly permissible until the authorities come knocking on the door.

Ambiguity is most evident in the relationships that develop in the workplace. After all, the fundamentals of leadership may be simple, but it is acting upon them as they relate to people and situations that leads to areas of gray, periods of uncertainty, and times of great stress. For example, employees want to know where they stand with their boss. Feedback is essential, but so often managers ignore the need, assuming incorrectly that the employee is doing fine so why tell him anything. Sounds dumb, but anyone who's worked in an organization for longer than a week knows that lack of feedback is a prime reason why people feel so uncertain. In turn, they turn their own personal uncertainty into a sense of ambiguity about the organization.

The job they have now may be just as good as any job, so they will be actively looking to move on, sooner than later. In this instance, ambiguity will cost organizations good people who are costly to replace in terms of recruitment, training, and retention. A little more clarity in the form of feedback may have avoided this situation, and it is a good example of where managers can remove ambiguity. Such measures then enable the leader and his team to focus on bigger ambiguities in the form of changing environments, conditions, and situations.

Learning to become comfortable with ambiguity is essential to leading from the middle; the sense of comfort may in time make up for the lack of ease managers feel when they don't have all of the data but have the confidence to move forward. Experienced managers know how to deal with uncertainty. Take, for example, an advertising agency. If you are an account manager and have been with the firm for more than five years, you have likely experienced the exhilarating highs of winning business and cold depths of losing a client. You have seen your clients trim your media budget in ways that make you wonder whether you can afford to hire a hand puppet for your next commercial. Working in an environment of unpredictability is the status quo.

The reassuring part of this equation is the people on your team. If you assess the talent on your team, you know that you have good people, ones with clever imaginations who can produce good work that customers will appreciate. In short, you have confidence that you and your team will survive, perhaps not as planned, but you will make it through. But you know equally well that your survival, and that of your people, requires to you ask questions, listen to what you hear and don't hear, and decide accordingly. Living with uncertainty is not fun, but it is something that good managers in the middle deal with and turn to their advantage as well as to the advantage of their people.

What You Need to Do to Push Back the Right Way

The boss needs someone who has the self-assurance to disagree with him or her. Bosses need straight talkers. Such people need to know their stuff as well as themselves. Such individuals need to balance the need of the boss to win with the need of the organization to win.

To push back the right way, you will need to:

- Develop your self-assurance.
- Tune your antennae to the situation.
- Know when to disagree and when to go with the flow.
- Provide your boss with timely feedback.
- Find comfort in uncertainty.

PART II

What Does the Team Need?

KNOWING YOUR TEAM IS a prerequisite for considering what it can do and how it will do it. An individual who leads up is likely to be a peer, not the boss, but he or she must think as a leader in order to get things done. Specifically, a peer leader knows how to give directions appropriately, influence people over whom he or she has no authority, and knows how to work the system in order to get things done.

LETTING OTHERS CREATE THE HOW

Never tell people how to do things. Tell them what to do and they will surprise you with their ingenuity.
GENERAL GEORGE S. PATTON, *WAR AS I KNEW IT*[1]

A good quote is like a punch to the solar plexus. It stops you in your tracks, and it metaphorically causes you to lose your breath with its profundity. The power of a good quote is really in its ability to make us think and reflect, and so it is with a quote about leadership that made me not only ponder, but challenged me to work out my own ideas about what it really meant. The author of the quote is someone who knew quite a bit about leadership, not from simply books, although he was an author and scholar mind you, but from having lived it.

He is James B. Stockdale, a Navy pilot whose plane was downed over North Vietnam in 1965, forcing him to spend more than seven years in a prison camp. Conditions were severe; torture was common. But through it all, courage prevailed. Stockdale was the highest ranking officer of the camp, dubbed by the inmates as the Hanoi Hilton. That gave him a de facto leadership position, but one that he earned by his example of courage and resilience.

Years after returning to America, Stockdale wrote books and became a researcher at the Hoover Institute studying Stoic philosophy.[2] Once, years after his release, the spotlight shone on him, unkindly it must be said, during the 1992 presidential campaign when as Ross Perot's vice presidential running mate he pondered a question during a debate in a philosophical manner in a way that made him seem confused and out of sorts. Stockdale deserved better, and this quote (a brilliant synthesis of three concepts) is a measure of his insight and reflects greatly on his understanding of the nature of leadership.[3]

"Leadership must be based on goodwill. Goodwill does not mean posturing and, least of all, pandering to the mob. It means obvious and wholehearted commitment to helping followers."

Goodwill is not a word heard much these days, so it rings on our ears with new meaning. It resonates with action, that is, you make goodness happen, not by chance but by choice, or will. Stockdale elaborates that goodwill is "wholehearted" and focused on "helping followers." That's what leadership is all about, service to others. So often managers either in the corporate or social sector forget this lesson, not because they are power mad or evil, but because they become so overwhelmed by the work that they forget the human quotient. A manager's job is about helping others do theirs, not out of altruism, but because that is the nature of management. A leader's job, however, does involve the heart and the commitment to service as a means of self-actualization as well as team realization.

"We are tired of leaders we fear, tired of leaders we love, and most tired of leaders who let us take liberties with them. What we need for leaders are men of heart who are so helpful that that they, in effect, do away with the need of their jobs."

Two things are going on in this statement. One is the weariness of tyranny in two forms, one of fear and the other of love. How can that be? Well, tyrants rule through terror, either institutional or personal brutality. At the same time, tyrants demand that people "love" them. Stalin, Mao, and Kim Jong Il come to mind with their cult of personality. They are at heart abusers not only of power, but of people. By contrast "leaders of the heart" are those who put people first. A leader who puts others ahead of self is one who leads physically from the front where he can be seen in times of strife, but leads metaphorically where he cannot be seen so that others share the credit for things that go well. In this sense, the leader has created conditions where people can lead themselves.

"But leaders like that are never out of a job, never out of followers. Strange as it sounds, great leaders gain authority by giving it away."

Imagine surrendering power to gain it. Stockdale is addressing the nature of influence whereby leaders gain in stature by demonstrating that power is not their endgame. George III understood this when he commented on George Washington's giving up command after his victory at Yorktown by saying that the general would become "the greatest man in the world." Washington, of course, came back to power and served two terms as president. In surrendering power as he did, twice, Washington set the standard for democratic leadership and gave our fledgling nation a legacy of authority backed by example.[4] For leaders today, Stockdale reminds us that the ultimate source of power is the example you leave to others.

Stockdale, who died in 2006, has come to prominence again as a seminal character in *Good to Great*. As Jim Collins relates in this book, he asks the admiral about those POWs in North Vietnam who did not return home. Stockdale replied, "The optimists." He explained that these were the fellows who kept thinking they would be released by Christmas, or Easter, or the next holiday. And when they were not released, they were crushed. "And they died of a broken heart." Collins fashioned this concept into something he called the Stockdale Paradox, which he defines as believing that you will succeed despite the obstacles, while at the same time acknowledging "the most brutal facts" facing you.[5] Stockdale did all of this and more in his lifetime, and as great men do, taught it to us not in words but by example.

What James Stockdale Teaches Us About Leading Up:

- Put the needs of others first.
- Lead by setting the right example.
- Exert courage in times of crisis.

■　■　■

Work Together

Every manager needs to set clear expectations for performance. For Admiral Stockdale, improved performance emerged from giving people authority to do their jobs without having to seek permission. Leaders who lead up gain in influence by giving their power away, and in return, the organization operates more effectively. However, in most organizations, performance is measured in two ways. One, what every employee must do in the job, that is, tasks and responsibilities. For example, if you work in purchasing, it will mean sending out bids, gathering information on potential suppliers, performing due diligence on vendors, and following established processes. For marketers, it may be developing the product position by conducting competitive analyses, researching customer wants and needs, and formulating marketing plans. Such expectations are clear and straightforward. Many managers in the middle work with their colleagues to develop the tasks and responsibilities because it gives employees a voice as well as keeps the manager in tune with what needs to be done.

The second part of the expectation process is the harder part, and the one that managers fail to articulate. It requires setting expectations for behavior, how employees conduct themselves in the workplace. Such expectations should be explicit and direct so that there is no guesswork. How each department conducts itself should be in line with the values and culture of the organization. And here is where middle managers can demonstrate real leadership; they can work with their direct reports, as Admiral Stockdale might advise, to share ownership of the job in order to get better results. Management, especially those in the middle, and employees can work together according to a model that boils down to three key elements, something I call the 3 Cs.

COORDINATE WITH OTHERS

Never assume that people will work together; make it known that it is a requirement. For example, the manager must make it clear that she expects people to coordinate on projects. Initially, the manager may have to spell out who does what and who reports what to whom. That's fine. Over time the information-sharing requirements will sort themselves out, and employees will determine what works best for them. But it is essential that the manager stays in the information loop for two reasons. One, she needs to know what is going on. Two, she needs to make certain that information is being shared. Until the practice of information sharing is established and demonstrated, employees will want to hoard it. It will be up to the manager to follow through on coordination.

COOPERATE

Every manager needs to communicate why employees need to cooperate. Cooperation within the team is the working together for a joint purpose. How an NFL football team shares information among staff and players serves as a good model. Videotape breakdowns of an upcoming opponent's games and plays are distributed to respective coaching staffs, offense and defense. Likewise, the coaching staffs view the tapes and show them to their players. In this way, critical information about the opponent is distributed, disseminated, and digested by those who need to know. Such cooperation is part and parcel of how teams cooperate off the field so they can cooperate more capably on the field when it matters most.

COLLABORATE

It is the sincere desire of every manager to have employees collaborate. Collaboration is the art and practice of two or more people pooling resources and talents to get the job done in a timely and efficient manner. The Tennessee Valley Authority provides a wonderful example of encouraging such collaboration. As part of its succession planning, veteran employees, often engineers with critical skills who are leaving TVA shortly, are teamed with young employees. Consider it a kind of mentor–mentee relationship where the vets teach the up-and-comers the tacit knowledge (that is, how things really work) required to do the job. For example, as reported in *Fortune* magazine, a senior engineer who had an uncanny knack for determining corrosion levels in pipes by tapping on them with a wrench was shadowed by a younger engineer who was presumably taught to do the same. Collaboration was critical.[6]

Make No Assumptions

While the 3C method for behavioral expectations makes common sense, some managers may fail to articulate it because they have been thrown into management without adequate preparation. Not to worry. This method can be used retroactively, as a means of conflict resolution. For example, say there is discord in the workplace, and the parties are at loggerheads. Get the two parties together and have each state his or her problem with the other. Easy to say, yes, but hard to implement, and mighty uncomfortable. But here's where coordination comes in; you make it clear that folks must coordinate together or find somewhere else to work. Once the venting is done, give them time to formulate a solution. This requires cooperation. Again, insist that it be done. And finally collaboration. The solution they develop will require folks working together, perhaps independently, but working at least for the good of the team. Coordination, cooperation, and collaboration can bring folks together if the manager stands behind the process.

There is one more advantage to articulating expectations for behavior. It avoids the "bad attitude" syndrome. The term is hurled around liberally but is often ill-defined, and as such, it often back-fires. By making it clear how you want folks to behave at work, you quantify behavior according to coordination, cooperation, and collaboration. Say someone is cutting people off or keeping others in the dark, you call him or her on that behavior. You say, "You are not cooperating" or "You are not collaborating." You focus not on personality, you focus on what the person is doing that is harmful and disruptive. Quantifying behavior by setting expectations is not being meddlesome, it's acting holistically for the benefit of the entire team. It gives the manager and the team expectations to live by and behaviors to emulate. Not a roadmap per se, but a plan of harmony that can make a positive difference.

Find the Right Fit

In his very first press conference, the young basketball coach demonstrated immediately why he was the right choice for the job. Charles Ramsey, a first-time head coach, stated, "You have to adapt to student athletes, it's a major part of coaching. We have to find out . . . what best fits them." This young coach demonstrated wisdom far beyond his years. Words like "adapt" and "fit" are not typical "coach speak." So much of coaching these days is hiring someone for his or her system. Ramsey has ideas, of course, but his first priority is the players already on the team.[7] Leverage the talent that you have and create a system where players can excel.

All too often organizations assign people jobs for which they are unsuited. For example, it puts accountants into sales jobs, engineers into marketing slots, or computer programmers into purchasing. Cross-functional development is fine and dandy, but it must be predicated on desire as well as suitability. A similar paradigm applies in management. The hierarchical nature of our management systems pushes people into management because they have excelled in their jobs. If expertise on the job were the only criteria, then all good accountants, designers, engineers, and finance people would be great managers. Sadly, we know this is not the case; management is its own discipline and must be mastered like any other competency.

Management is about getting the right results with the right people, but so often we may have the right people — competent, dedicated, and willing — but in the wrong slots. Success depends on the right people, in the right positions, and voila, you get the right results. Easy to state, of course, but so many middle managers must work with the talent they inherit. They must find ways to maximize that talent in order to achieve organizational goals. Here are some suggestions.

ASSESS WHAT YOU HAVE

Baseball teams have spring training; football teams have camp. The purpose of both is the same: Find out what talent you have, develop game plans around that talent, and trade for talent you need. Baseball teams always can use another good pitcher; football teams can typically use another running back or pass blocker. Managers need to find out what the people on their team like to do and do well. If someone likes to work alone and is conscientious, give her assignments where attention to detail is essential. On the other hand, those who are sociable and like working in teams are natural collaborators; create team projects.

ADAPT YOUR APPROACH

So often, managers cannot draft the talent they need. Frequently, they get what is delegated to them. The challenge for the manager is to adapt to the talent she has. For example, if you have a group of diligent task-oriented employees, you will need to provide them some direction, but not a great deal. On the other hand, if your team is highly creative and focused on big-picture concerns, you will need to find ways to get them to focus on work at hand. You will be managing them closely. Adapt your style and devise work strategies that suit your people. Output is essential, but every so often a few tweaks here or there, with the support of the employees, will not simply increase productivity, it will send it soaring.

OFFER OPPORTUNITY

Put people into positions where they can succeed. That may mean you need to provide additional training, cross-functional assignments, and job rotations. It also dictates that you recruit talent to your team who complement your style and your team. This does not mean you hire clones of yourself; you hire for opposites — people who do what you and your team cannot do well. When you have the right people in place, you can create a system that maximizes everyone's abilities.

Consider the People Quotient

Yes, people should come first in every organization, but not all of the time. The role of a company is to serve its customers and in the process deliver a healthy return so it can pay its employees fair and just compensation. Yet we do not operate in textbook environments; we compete in a global economy where faster, better, and cheaper rules. The human equation is sadly cast aside when another company, across the street or more frequently across the globe, can better meet emerging customer demands. Employees must understand this conundrum and do what they can to prepare themselves to find alternate forms of employment or be willing to learn new skills in order to become more valuable employees.

Putting the right people into the right positions is a leadership behavior. It demands that managers let people know what is expected and how they must perform. If they can do the work, fine. If they cannot, or will not, then management should try to find alternate positions when possible. It may be in an adjacent department, or it may require the help of outplacement services. Keeping the misfits does no one any favors; it becomes a breeding ground for discontent that can poison the workplace for all. At the same time, finding ways to adapt a system to the worker's abilities creates an environment where individuals and teams can excel.

Just Ask!

John Madden, football broadcaster extraordinaire, told a story about a contentious player who had just joined his new team. While the player was talented, he had a reputation of not being a team player. In the course of the conversation with coaches of his new team, the player was asked what his expectations were. This question had a twofold effect: It welcomed the player to the team, and also put the player on notice that his expectations for success must meld with team expectations.[8]

Madden's story imparts a terrific lesson. Managers are taught from day one to set clear expectations for their people; such expectations include not only objectives but expectations for behavior. All too often managers may neglect to ask their employees their expectations, that is, what they expect to get out of the job in terms of productivity as well as job enrichment. As Madden's story illustrates, when you ask an employee, you shift some of the burden of management solely from the shoulders of the coach, or manager, to the shoulders of the player, or employee. Asking employees about their expectations accomplishes two things: One, you have the opportunity to find out about them as people and performers; and two, you enfranchise the individual into the organization, that is, you give him or her a reason to share.

Asking is a form of questioning, of course. It can be used to find out information, but it carries a much broader scope. Asking denotes respect; it demonstrates that manager cares enough about his people to want to know something about them. Asking in the form of a request is a form of invitation. You are asking for participation. In this way asking becomes a behavior that managers can employ to build trust and drive results. Asking, of course, is a form of communication, and it exacts responsibilities for both managers and employees.

For managers seeking to lead up, asking is a form of bringing people into the business at hand and keeping them engaged in the process. Here are some ways to do that.

ASK FOR EXPECTATIONS

As John Madden's story illustrates, asking an employee about what he expects in his job is both a welcome as well as a notice. When you ask an employee to tell you what he expects in his job, you gain an insight into what he hopes to accomplish. You get past the resume and delve into motivation. The more a manager knows about his employee, the better he can communicate and relate to him on level that engages the employee's desires as well as expectations. At the same time, you may learn that the employee is not right for the job. Better to learn this up front than down the line in the middle of a project.

ASK FOR IDEAS

Management is not a solo act, although some managers feel they must do it all by themselves. Managers arrive at such notions for a variety of reasons, e.g., desire for total control or, conversely, fear of letting go. Neither reason is healthy; both lead to managerial burnout as well as employee turnoff.

ASK FOR SUPPORT

Chris Matthews, whom we met earlier, tells the story of his former boss, Speaker of the House, Tip O'Neill. An enormously successful and popular politician, O'Neill learned a hard lesson in his first electoral contest; he was seeking to be a councilman for Cambridge City Council. A neighbor woman told him that she was intending to vote for him despite the fact that he had not asked her to do so. O'Neill protested that he had always helped this woman out, cutting her lawn and shoveling her walk. To which she replied, "Tom, I want you to know something: People like to be asked."[9] Indeed! When managers ask their employees, they are inviting them to contribute as well as share the leadership load. Yes, it is true that people are hired to do a job and may not need to be asked, but when you make the effort to ask, you demonstrate that you value the individual as a person, not simply as a drone.

Engage by Asking

Asking is also a form of engagement. For those seeking to lead their bosses and their peers, it demonstrates that you are willing to do your part to keep the enterprise going. For example:

Ask What You Can Do

John Kennedy famously asked, "Ask not what your country can do for you, but what you can do for your country." There is a lesson for employees in that statement. Look for ways to help out; do not always expect to be told what to do. Look for opportunities to add value to your department's workflow, and by doing so, grow your own skills. Pitching in without being told demonstrates the flip side of the ask proposition, e.g., you are willing to be a team player likely because you have been treated well and regularly asked to contribute.

Ask for Feedback

Employees have a right to feedback because it provides them with an assessment of their performance. Managers owe it to their employees to deliver good news and bad. While many managers may be tempted to deliver feedback only at appraisal time, that is shortsighted. Feedback must be frequent and ongoing. And likewise, managers should invite their employees to provide feedback on their management style. When both manager and employee partake in this give and take, they not only come to know one another better, they can work more efficiently because they have a foundation based upon shared knowledge and trust.

Ask Not the Impossible

As desirable a practice as asking may become, it is not always feasible. In times of crisis, leaders in the middle may not have much time to ask people about their hopes and dreams, they must ask for information and then give orders. There is nothing wrong with that. Later, when things calm down, managers can shift into a more participatory mood and engage one on one.

Asking is a fine habit. It fosters bonds of trust between manager and employee, especially when asking becomes a reciprocal behavior with each party free to ask the other. You can look at asking as facilitating five things, all of which coincidentally happen to begin with the letter "C." Asking sparks *courtesy*; people are more respectful of one another. Asking breeds *comity*; people get along with each other. Asking fosters *cooperation*; when people tolerate one another, they can more easily work together. Asking leads to *commitment*; people want to contribute to the work and to one another. And finally, asking builds *community*; people who get along and work together develop strong ties not only to the work but to one another in both good and bad times. Taken as one, those five things make for one powerful workforce that can accomplish great things. All it takes is a little asking.

Hold Back on Solutions

One of the hardest things for smart people to do is to shut up. Michael Szwarcbord, general manager of Flinders Medical Centre in Adelaide, Australia, made this point in a presentation he delivered on implementing lean thinking in his hospital. The tendency of people at the top, especially those with credentials, is to provide answers to every question. Doctors especially follow this guideline; after all, it is in their training. You don't go to a doctor to have him tell you, "I don't know." But when it comes to implementing organizational change, the "don't know" answer may be the best answer. Szwarcbord refers to this as "no solutions thinking." His colleague, Sue O'Neill, executive director of nursing, seconded this idea. When it comes to change initiatives such as lean, you need people who can "reform, implement, and lead" — as O'Neill puts it. If you want that reform to stick and be implemented, you need people who can lead from the trenches. And that's where the thinking part comes in. Give people the opportunity to do their own problem solving.[10]

Not providing solutions applies not simply to healthcare but to leadership in general. So much of our management requires hierarchy; those at the top tell everyone else what to do. While this structure is good for setting direction, it is less good in actually doing the work. Why? Because people at the top are not involved in daily operations. Those in middle management are responsible for designing products, keeping the books, selling the products, or serving customers, Their job is to supervise in the truest sense, that is, provide guidance for others to follow.

Middle managers are those challenged with solving thorny issues, but like their senior leaders, they cannot do it by themselves. And so for them, standing back and holding fire is a good course of action. But, more important, this practice encourages people doing the work to think for themselves. That may be the greatest benefit of all. So how can middle managers encourage the "hold your fire" management model? Here are some suggestions.

ENCOURAGE THINKING

We are a culture that values action and results — that is, you must do something to get something. It is a powerful mantra and it works. However, sometimes action leads folks into blind alleys. Look at the number of "me-too" products that proliferate. Companies introduce them as stop-gap measures to protect a niche. In general, such products only clutter the marketplace. They also drain resources from the "me-too makers," resources that could be applied to internally derived innovations. To say no to the clone product requires a degree of big-picture thinking that looks at the long-term consequences. Thinking should be encouraged prior to every staff meeting; ask people to bring new ideas to the table.

ASK QUESTIONS FOR INFORMATION

Managers who like to be in charge are valuable to the organization; they demonstrate they have the autonomy to succeed. But so much of management is about delegation that too much "in charge" can thwart people's demonstrating initiative. When a problem arises, the manager should not be the first to speak. Look to others to step in. If no one speaks up, the manager can ask probing questions such as What is happening? Why we are doing this? How can we do better? and What should we do next? Asking these questions to elicit information (rather than assign blame) will stimulate good discussion.

MAP YOUR PROCESSES

One method of surfacing issues and problems is to ask people to process map, that is, to depict what they do in terms of input, flow, and output. Anyone with a science or technical background takes to such mapping like a duck to water; their enthusiasm will bring the nontechnical types into the mix. By depicting issues pictorially, you can arrive at deeper understandings of issues and problems. This was a technique that the team at Flinders Medical Centre employed to great advantage. The key is to get people to do the mapping themselves; the physical activity will naturally encourage broad participation as well as stimulate deeper levels of understanding.

Hand Over the No-No/Go Switch

All too often when roadblocks appear, employees will look to management to deal with them. Work stops in its tracks. Take a product development group. If customer feedback on prototypes shows that customers have a preference for one feature or another, all too often, designers will stand back and wait for management to decide. Decisions, however, may not be forthcoming; time to market may be wasted. Therefore, it may be better for the development team to make its own decisions based on customer need and in balance with the value proposition (that is, quality, cost, and profit considerations). By turning over the decision making to the team, managers demonstrate responsibility and accountability.

Defer to the Top

Giving authority to front-line people to make decisions is fine for most situations, but not all. Leadership is often most about making the toughest of the tough decisions; that is, where you require people of experience and the vantage point to look at the whole picture. For example, when two teams are competing for resources to implement their ideas, only someone in a position of authority over both can make the decision about who gets resources. One of the parties will be pleased; the other crushed. But the decision maker has to find a way to keep both sides focused and engaged on the process.

For the most part, however, not offering a solution in day-to-day situations, or even throughout the implementation of a change initiative, is a good thing. Proof of this comes from watching lean initiatives unfurl and take hold in healthcare. As indicated by the example of Flinders hospital and others like it around the world, it is the nurses who make things happen; they know the patients as well as the doctors, not to mention the system. They are close to the action but have their heart in the game, e.g., improve patient care. Nurses are the key differentiators in lean initiatives in healthcare. Their example can teach those of us who wince at the sight of needles, let alone blood, how to implement change. It is often by letting go of established hierarchy and trusting well-trained and well-intentioned people to decide for themselves. That is leading up in action.

Foster the EQ Connection

Far too many of us have suffered in jobs with managers who combine the compassion of Soviet party bosses with the warmth of Vlad the Impaler. Such hard-charging executives suffer from a lack of adequate leadership EQ, the emotional intelligence to engage the hearts and minds of followers. In other words, their competencies as managers do not overcome their incompetencies as leaders. Their inability to rally others to their side is a real detriment. When you look into your own experiences, you discern a pattern: bosses who put themselves before others. Emotional intelligence as it applies to leadership requires a willingness to understand the needs of others and deliver on them in ways that benefit the organization. Anyone seeking to lead from the middle must find ways to cultivate emotional intelligence. Here are three ways.

Connect as a Human Being

Rank may have privileges, but leaders who stand on it alone will be just that — alone! Leaders need to communicate in ways that convey their values and beliefs as well as their commitment to the organization. Sometimes connection takes the form of presenting an idea and taking questions; other times it is as simple as making small talk in ways that put people at ease. It is the connection that matters.

Check for Understanding

One-way communications are good for street signs but not for interpersonal communications. Good leaders discipline themselves to ask questions to make certain people understand. They also are adept at reading facial expressions, and when they are met by furrowed brows, skeptical glances, or blank looks, they pause and find out why. Understanding occurs from a back-and-forth exchange.

SHARE WHAT YOU HAVE

Trust is earned by example. When people see their leader sharing information and resources, or making changes requested by employees, they develop a connection that in time leads to trust. Sometimes the sharing takes the form of coaching, as when a manager pulls aside a new hire to explain a process or give a lesson in corporate protocol and does it in ways that make the employee feel good about herself.

Give of Yourself

The operative principle in connecting, understanding, and sharing is the giving of self; that is, putting others first. Good leaders give of themselves because they have something to give; their sense of self both in terms of confidence as well as ability is big enough to share. And it is ultimately in the sharing that a leader makes the connection. Examples of such sharing can be found in thousands of diaries and letters penned by British troops during World War I. These writings contain countless stories of officers in the trenches going from soldier to soldier prior to a climb "over the top" into No Man's Land. This connection made soldier to soldier, man to man, was genuine, and often the last measure for both since such attacks incurred such fearsome casualty figures.[11]

Emotional intelligence in itself does not make for enlightened leadership. Some managers who relate well to others may lack the resolve to lead others. They may be unwilling to make tough decisions about people, such as promotions, job transfers, or even terminations, for fear of hurting others' feelings. These sentiments are admirable human qualities but may be harmful to leaders who must make hard decisions on issues like facility relocations and layoffs. Furthermore, in times of crisis, organizations demand a strong hand on the tiller; they need the leader who can look over the choppy seas and see land. Crisis leadership demands people of strong constitution and strong will. They are not autocrats who rule by fiat and fear; they are managers who lead by values, principles, and personal example.

Emotional intelligence is the human face of leadership, and it is especially critical to those who are leading up. That humanity makes it possible for leaders to connect with subordinates and superiors alike. Emotional intelligence can create a sense of inspired leadership, the kind that will make people want to go the extra mile because it is good for them, their leader, and their organization.

Compromise

A strong sense of self can open the doors to understanding alternate points of view. So often news coming from Washington these days reflects the discord of politicians who seem to hold tighter to their ideology than they do to constituent concerns. Civility and collaboration among political adversaries greased the wheels of the U.S. political process for much of the twentieth century. No longer. Given the polarity of the U.S. electorate, compromise has come to be equated with selling out. Comity between adversaries has gone by the wayside. By contrast, business demonstrates in many ways how to prosper through compromise. In a free market society, conceiving, developing, and delivering a product or service is filled with hundreds of compromises that balance the needs of the consumer to obtain value with the needs of the producer to make a profit.

Compromise is not a betrayal of values; it is an agreement over a position where both sides come away with something to their liking. Not every compromise is a good one. General Motors' compromise with its unions over health and pensions has resulted in legacy costs of at least $1,400 per vehicle; that was a contributing factor to GM's financial collapse that required the intervention of the federal government and bankruptcy to save it. On the other hand, compromise between oil producers and the environmentalists has resulted in the implementation of drilling methods that are more ecologically compatible as well as the creation and preservation of natural habitats.

Compromise ensures the common interest. As such it is a valuable practice for managers who seek to lead up to learn and implement. Why? Because compromise is a means by which the talent and skills of a diverse team can be harnessed for the completion of a project. Compromise ensures that people participate, and their collaboration overcomes not only inertia but also resistance. Here are some ways to encourage compromise.

INSIST ON COLLABORATION

Reflect for a moment on your most positive team experience. It may be something that occurred in high school athletics, or you may be experiencing it right now in your workplace. If you consider why the team succeeded, it is due not simply to the individual proficiencies of teammates, but it was everyone's ability to meld together, not always as friends, but as collaborators who respect one another's talents and abilities. That's teamwork, and in a larger picture it is the collaboration of individuals for the greater good, e.g., producing intended results in the form of winning games or winning in the marketplace. How can managers insist on collaboration? The first way is through example. Make it known that you are willing to share the hardships, be it longer hours or more difficult assignments. A second way is through open and honest communications. Set clear expectations and be available to listen and learn from others on the team.

LEVERAGE DISSENT

The job of employees is not to agree with the boss 100 percent of the time. Employees should feel free to offer alternate points of view about how the work is done or about the intended results. At the same time, managers have a right to expect that the work will be done on time and on budget. Managers may also insist on adherence to standards of quality and practice and exact discipline when those metrics are not met. But within that framework there is room for dissent. Creative tension over ideas provokes good thinking and rigorous analysis. The development of marketing campaigns resembles a laboratory for collaborative thinking. Product offering and research are combined with lots of clever minds to develop strategies and creative solutions that make the offering desirable, accessible, and available to the consumer, be it a company or an individual. Managers can encourage dissent through the process of appreciative inquiry — that is, the asking of questions designed to elicit different ideas as well as affirm rights of people who want to ask questions.

SEEK COMITY

One of the reasons people shy away from compromise is because they feel it is not worth jeopardizing team harmony. True to a degree, perhaps, but team unity is threatened more seriously by failure to compromise. When individuals on a team are competing among themselves to deliver on a project, it is psychologically wearing. As mentioned above, creative tension can be a positive, but emotional tension erodes comity and provokes disagreements and disputes that are directed at personalities rather than projects. It therefore falls to the manager to assuage egos and soothe hard feelings. Compromises where parties share in the process as well as the rewards will make the workplace more harmonious. Sometimes gratification will be deferred. Surrender on one point may not deliver a personal gain, but it will demonstrate that the individual has the strength of character to be a good team player. Such recognition may be the most valuable outcome of compromise.

Show Strength Through Compromise

As valued as compromise may be to organizational health, there are two instances, at least, where compromise can be damaging. The first instance is ethics. When you compromise over hiring someone with a questionable background, or look the other way over a suspect invoice or inflated expense report, you eat away at the integrity of the organization. Just as one bad apple will spoil the barrel, one bad actor can damage the reputation of an organization and do it irreparable harm. A second instance is values, which are defined as the truths and beliefs that bind people to an organization. When athletes dope themselves to enhance performance, values are thrown by the wayside because dopers violate the spirit of their sport as well as the sanctity of competition. They tilt the playing field to the detriment of fellow athletes, spectators, and themselves. Everyone loses.

Compromise is considered an art because it does not result from a process diagram or an employee handbook; genuine compromise emerges from looking to the hearts and minds of your people to find best possible solutions. Ideally, compromise creates win-win situations, but not always. Sometimes the one who compromises the most is the one who has the most to lose. For example, a project manager who is willing step back from the team and allow others to add their ideas, as well as their labor, to make the project come along may be sacrificing her own pet ideas for the good of the whole. That is compromise of the highest order. And it is also known by another name — leadership from the middle!

Overcome Distrust

Leadership, however, requires strong trust to flourish. A guy I know once told me that one of the reasons he left his company was because he suspected that its management was not always straight with its employees. Research by Watson Wyatt, a leading human resource consultancy, shows that my friend is not alone in this kind of thinking. A majority of employees feel that management is not always trustworthy. Lack of trust is fundamental to organizational health, and it's not simply for show. According to a study by Towers Perrin, another HR consulting firm, when people are engaged in their work (and trust is essential to feeling engaged), they feel they can have a positive impact on quality and service and are more likely to stay with their company. It's common sense really; surveys merely confirm what is obvious. But the other question is what to do when distrust outweighs trust. It is harder to overcome distrust than it is to build trust.[12]

Beginning with a clean slate is an optimal situation; the manager gets the benefit of the doubt with his team. People want him to succeed and will pull their weight until the manager gives them reason to do otherwise. However, in situations where the manager is taking over a dysfunctional department, or has himself caused his team to lose trust, then the situation is far more difficult. In the first instance, the manager must establish new ground rules; she sets expectations for performance as well as behavior. Determining objectives is only the half of it; she must also discuss what she expects in terms of coordination, cooperation, and collaboration. For employees who have endured an "every person for him- or herself climate," the idea of working in harmony with others will seem airy-fairy. That's where the manager must insist on it and lead by example. He will have to work with others soliciting input, building consensus, and sometimes pitching in to do the tough jobs. Most will follow the boss's example. Those who do not get the message will need to move onto to other jobs. Sometimes removing one malcontent will improve the attitude and outlook of the entire team.

So often, for middle managers inheriting dysfunctional teams, instilling trust can be time consuming, but it is not as hard as trying to rebuild trust with a team that is suffering from your missteps. For example, say your team does a good job and makes deadline under incredible pressure. So you stand up and take credit for their hard work, rather than sharing the spotlight with your team. Bad move, but there can be redemption. And here are some suggestions for beginning to rebuild trust.

Be Open

Admit you screwed up. Apologize for hogging credit, or doing whatever it was you did to lose the trust of your team. Do not make excuses; be straight and open. Such an admission at the next staff meeting would be a good gesture, but it's only the first step. You must accept responsibility and hold yourself accountable. Talk about ways to regain trust. Listen to what people tell you and use their words as starting points.

Turn It Around

Find a way to make it up to the team. For example, if you failed to give recognition, make time to do it immediately. When people do a job well, let them know. Better yet, let your supervisors know, too. Publicize the milestones the team achieves. Celebrate their accomplishments.

Prove It

Words are one thing; actions are another. Not only make a habit of sharing the credit, but make it a habit to share the tough stuff, too. Be available to pitch in for the heavy lifting. Ask people how you can help them. Often that will mean finding more resources or going to bat for them in front of senior management. Standing up for your team where they can see you do it sends a powerful message that you are trying to make a positive difference. Rebuilding trust is never easy, but it is worth doing and it can engender an even greater sense of loyalty.

Know That Compromise Is Not Always Possible

Despite these good intentions, there are managers who are beyond redemption. And as one who leads up, you need to be aware of their shortcomings. For example, the manager who mismanages time, resources, and people so that a project fails, yet he points the finger at others, is even more loathsome. Such a manager shows by example that his interests come first. Regaining trust will be next to impossible. Coaching may be an option, but if the manager is that self-absorbed, he is unlikely to admit mistakes on his own. He may be incapable of change, and for that reason, coaching is not worth the investment.

Trust is essential to the organization; it is what holds people to the organization. And while we may want and expect our senior leaders to be trustworthy, they may fail us from time to time. Those we turn to will be our peers. Such a practice is common on the battlefield. Soldiers fight for flag and country, but they suffer, bleed, and die for the soldier next to them. This fact has been true in every war from ancient times to the current conflict. Why is this so? Human nature dictates that we trust those we can see, touch, feel, and understand. And who better than the person next to us? Working in cubicle is not the same as walking patrol, but the same instinct of self-preservation as well as desire to do a job and do it well is universal. That can only come from trust. And so we must be open to trusting others as we expect them to trust us. Live it real, and the trust will come.

Communicate Teamwork

Trust can never be imposed; it is earned. And not simply from leader to follower, but also from follower to follower, that is, leading your colleagues. As discussed earlier, management requires matching talents and skills to assignments. One of the leading reasons that people fail at work is because they are doing work that is not suited to them. This failure is compounded when you put people on teams that do not click or people simply do not get along. Sometimes there is no choice, but often with some skillful people skills, managers can play to their strengths and overcome the deficiencies. One leading automotive company devoted a great deal of time and energy to team coaching — finding ways to team people of varying talents and skills but find ways for them to put their best foot forward. The results were an award-winning series of products that established new levels of excellence in performance and styling.

The key to team harmony is open and frequent communication. This does not mean that everyone has to be buddy buddy; you are organizing a team to do a job, not enjoy a party. Celebrations may occur, but only when people click as professionals. Toward that end, it is up to the middle manager as team leader to ensure that communications genuinely occurs. Here are some suggestions to make certain it happens.

SELECT WISELY

The success of a project depends largely on the team. Managers can often determine success or failure right from the start by selecting people who complement one another. Sometimes managers think they need to pack a team with stars, men and women who have demonstrated superior abilities. This may work, but often it does not. To lead as a middle manager, you need role players, those who can fill in the gaps and do what is necessary to bring out the best in the superstars.

REMEMBER THAT OPPOSITES ATTRACT

When forming a team, look for complementary talents. As Stephen Covey has written, "Strength lies in differences, not in similarities." Advertising agencies excel in teaming opposites; in fact, the teaming of creatives with account managers is a blend of opposition in itself. By why limit this to marketing? For example, if you are developing a logistics system, the type of people engaged in the project will be focused, detail driven, and systems oriented. Is there any rule that says you cannot employ an outside-the-box thinker, too? This can be an individual who understands the project but who can periodically challenge assumptions as a means of developing something special that not only fulfills need, but exceeds expectations.

FOCUS ON HARMONY

Teams find a rhythm to their work and slowly but surely begin to pick up steam. In communication terms, they begin to find their own voice. Teammates learn shorthand; sometimes a word, a gesture, or even a wink says more than a report. A word such as "Why" from a team leader can provoke a rethinking of an idea. Likewise, a wink from that person can assure the individual that she's on the right track. Harmony emerges from people who share the same goals and strive to reach them.

PROMOTE DISSENT

As much as you want teams to harmonize, you want them to challenge themselves. Not everyone on the team must be friends, but they must be collaborators. But collaboration does not mean teammates must check their brains at the door. No way! Some of the best teams are those that challenge the status quo. The challenge is not to the person but to an idea. Managers need to encourage thinking, often thinking that is contrary to the mainstream ideas of the team. Why? Because when there is tension over ideas, it means that people are considering what they are doing and why they are doing it. Of course, if this dissent corrupts relationships, it is destructive, but when channeled appropriately, it can be rewarding.

Get the Job Done

As much as managers in the middle might strive for team harmony, there are many times when reality dictates that the job comes first. In other words, managers must ask their folks to put up and shut up. Such occasions occur when resources are tight, manpower is in short supply, and time is of the essence. Crises provoke urgency, and managers must act first and play to the gallery later. Take the example of an engineer responsible for quality improvement who inherits a project that is floundering. The best way forward is to ask the team what they would suggest and then implement their ideas quickly, together with the manager's own best ideas. When the project is righted, the manager who leads up can focus on the human equation.

Leaders who lead up know that a team is only as successful as the individuals on it. Together they must be stronger as a whole than as individuals. Ray Kroc, the founder of McDonald's, preached team from the restaurant up through franchise relations. He mandated operational efficiencies, but let the franchises focus on marketing and new product innovation. McDonald's in Kroc's day was a balance between system efficiency and individual contributions.[13] It is a model the company emulates today, and a model that works for teams of any size and any endeavor. Another entrepreneur, Andrew Carnegie, put it this way: "Teamwork . . . is the fuel that allows common people to attain uncommon results." When people feel they are contributing, they feel better about themselves as well as their teammates and they accomplish their goals individually and collectively.

What You Need to Do to Let Others Create the How

The team needs direction, but it does not always need mile markers. That means leaders need to set direction, but then step back and let people discover for themselves *how* to get things done. When people learn how, they are motivated to take more ownership and in turn share what they've learned with others.

To let others create the how, you will need to:
- Set expectation for behavior (as well as performance).
- Find the right people for the right jobs.
- Make an art of compromise.
- Communicate teamwork (live it, too).
- Insist on ownership and accountability.

BREAKING DOWN THE DOORS

All your power is in your people. Your job is enabling
everybody to contribute to their fullest.

ALAN MULLALLY, CEO, FORD MOTOR COMPANY[1]

Some rock stars make headlines for bad behavior. Others occasionally make news by endorsing a candidate or a cause. Bono, lead singer for the Irish band U2, eschews headlines in favor of action. His mission is dealing with the plagues that threaten the social, cultural, and economic fabric of Africa — AIDS and poverty. His solutions are debt relief and government-sponsored foreign aid. "This isn't a cause. We all have our causes," Bono said, "This is an emergency." One Campaign, which he helped to found with others, is an organization pledged to help Africa.[2]

"Rock stars are good at making noise," says Bono, who knows how to turn on the charm, too. His nickname derived from a hearing aid store in his native Dublin called Bonavox, Latin for "beautiful voice." He says, "I'm an activist. . . . [D]eep down I'm very serious about these things and I'm very angry." Such determination enabled him to persevere with his musical career. "We formed a band before we could play our instruments." What held them together was "humor" and "a sense of what [we] are against more than what [we] are for." Such bonds held them together in tough times; while they were known in Ireland; their reputation did not precede them to London. Nine people showed up for one of their early gigs in London. Still, it did not take long for word, via their music, to spread and by the mid 1980s, they were a major musical force. That opened the door for U2 to perform at the 1985 Live Aid concert, followed by the "Conspiracy of Hope" tour for Amnesty International.[3]

Having navigated the jagged shoals of the music business and prospered handsomely to enjoy financial security and critical acclaim, Bono is applying those same skills to raising awareness and funds for Africa's neediest. After all, how many rock stars can persuade the then-Secretary of the Treasury in the Bush Administration Paul O'Neill to tour Africa with him to see what the U.S. government can do to help? As expected, Bono meets with people on the Democratic side, Bill Clinton and John Kerry. But he also was invited to meet with President George W. Bush as well as the late Jesse Helms, a virulently right-wing critic of aid for social causes. Helms actually apologized to Bono for his past actions, admitting he had been wrong about AIDS and that the United States needed to help Africa in her hour of need. Add to that, Bono met with Pope Paul II; they traded gifts. The Pope gave Bono a rosary; Bono gave the Pontiff a pair of his sunglasses, which he duly showed off for the cameras. As a social realist, Bono does not impose litmus tests on people who can help; Africa needs support of people from all political stripes.[4]

Hobnobbing and lobbying are one thing. Bono spends time on the ground. It has made him a realist. One of the reasons that AIDS is such a scourge in Africa is that it creates a stigma that leads to denial. Truck drivers' nomadic existence and patronizing of prostitutes helped spread HIV from area to area. Bono is sanguine about his prospects. "No one is doing a good enough job . . . . I have myself seen people queuing up to die, three in a bed, two on top, one underneath."[5] Still Bono perseveres.

Ever the political realist, Bono is leveraging America's image abroad as a reason for assisting Africa. "Brand USA has taken some blows and some knocks. And I'm saying there is an opportunity here." For Bono that "opportunity" is to provide aid to eradicate poverty and disease and at the same time reaffirm the U.S. position as a moral force for good, as it was in Europe during the Marshall Plan. Such action would serve as a bulwark against terrorism; and there is another benefit. "It's cheaper than fighting wave after wave of terrorists' new recruits." Bono sees America as having no other choice. "God is not going to accept [refusal to help] as answer, and history is not going to accept that as an answer either."[6,7]

In 2005, *Time* named Bono a Person of the Year, along with philanthropists Bill and Melinda Gates. As the world's richest man, Gates does not go out of his way to meet with celebrities. Bono was a different matter; Gates sensed not only Bono's dedication to the cause of eradicating poverty in Africa with his One Campaign but also his command of data to support his arguments. "He just happens to be a geek who's a fantastic musician," says Gates, something of an ubergeek himself. Jesse Helms told *Time*, "I knew as soon as I met Bono that he was genuine. . . . In fact, he has opened himself to criticism because he has been willing to work with anyone [like a Helms] to find help for these children who have taken his heart."[8]

As a working class lad from Dublin, Bono understands that a world in which "celebrity is currency" gives him a stage upon which to preach. He happily accepts his calling. "The word 'duty' is an old-fashioned one, but I think we may have to just think about the word 'duty' again. This is a duty and a privilege."[9]

What Bono Teaches Us About Leading Up:

- Develop your confidence by becoming expert in what you do.
- Leverage confidence to accomplish good in another discipline.
- Network with people in high places to effect positive change.

■ ■ ■

Bono is someone who knows how to use his influence to succeed. He knows how to make himself and his ideas heard, even by people who may be predisposed to dislike him. Yet he wins them over by virtue of his personal commitment and ability to persuade others of the righteousness of his cause. Bono has met with success because he knows how to break down the doors. He does it through the power of his influence, something that everyone who desires to lead his boss and peers must learn.

Understand Means of Influence

Experts who have studied influence from a behavior standpoint posit that influence comes down to two dichotomous strands: *push* and *pull*. Push indicates someone is forcing or compelling, typically by virtue of position or authority. Those on the receiving end must accept what is being offered. For example, a general who issues an order expects it to be obeyed; his rank ensures compliance. Likewise a CEO mandates an initiative, and through his authority it will be developed and pushed through the system, at least for a little while. Push is rooted in power. Pull, on the other, implies persuasion, typically where the person pulling has little or no authority. The other party who is being influenced has the right of refusal. An engineer responsible for implementing a lean manufacturing process might fall into this category. While the initiative has been blessed from on high, it is up to the engineer to ensure acceptance, compliance, and ultimately commitment of people who must implement it. Pull is based on persuasion. Both power and persuasion are forms of influence; both are important tools in the process of leading up.[10]

Central to influence is change; it is the fulcrum by which leaders drive change. Why else would you need to influence if not for change? Leaders in the middle need to be front and center on anticipating, adapting, and embracing change. Influence is the means they use to bring others to accept it. Even when leaders push for stability, they are advocating a form of change, that is, the acceptance of what is. To win over others, a leader may employ one or more of seven (at least) different styles. Let's list them:

1. *Information* refers to the dissemination of data to make the case. Arguments based on facts are the bedrock of persuasion. Information when properly gathered and presented forms the foundation for influence to occur. You can refer to this foundation as the business case, that is, the logic for what you are arguing and why. Reports via speech or email are a key means of dissemination information. [Shorthand term: Just the facts.]

2. *Charisma* is a reflection of leadership presence. More than charm, it is the leader's appeal to an individual or group. It is a form of confidence that brings people to the leader and makes them happy to be persuaded. Influence based on charisma will position the leader as the champion of the idea or the initiative. He will carry the appeal of the argument to others. [Shorthand term: Sex appeal.]

3. *Participation* is the engagement of others in the act of influence. It is a viable tactic because it opens influence to others. Few leaders can, or ultimately should, persuade by themselves. They need allies to help carry the argument as well as to make the case. Participation relies upon involvement, especially involvement in a cause larger than oneself, such as developing a new product or service, or participating in a political or civil movement. [Shorthand term: All together now.]

4. *Compromise* is the bringing together of different or divergent points to view. Put simply, compromise is when both sides give up something to gain something. True enough, one side may give more than another, but when it comes to influence, compromise facilitates good feelings as well as the notion that both sides win. Compromise depends upon

the willingness of others to listen as well as to check for understanding. It requires a degree of discipline as well as a willingness to pay attention to other people's needs. [Shorthand term: Win/win.]

5. *Reason* is the tool of logic. Appeals to reason are pitches to the intellect. This works well in situations when people can agree with and accept the business case. It works less well when people are emotionally involved, in particular when people feel they are losing out or must give up something. Reason forms the basis of most business cases; it is the quantitative argument for making change or not making it. [Shorthand term: Why we do what we do.]

6. *Emotional appeal* appeals to the heart. Any successful change initiative must appeal to the heart; that is, people need to know and feel the WIFM, the "what's in it for me." Arguments based on emotion engage the heart; they work well with issues near and dear to individuals. Such arguments work less well when people do not have much stake in the outcome. People feel the emotional appeal, and that is good when change works to the benefit of the organization. It does just the opposite when people sense that they are losing out, be it their autonomy, responsibility, or even their job. [Shorthand term: Make 'em cry.]

7. *Coercion* is the ultimate application of force. It is the imposition of rank and privilege in order to get things done. Used appropriately, that is, to ensure compliance with things of significant magnitude such as the law or ethical codes, it is vital. Used indiscriminately, coercion becomes a weapon in the hands of people who lack the skill or will to engage people voluntarily. There is another use for coercion: When an enterprise is failing and no other alternatives are viable, it may be appropriate for those at the top to mandate strict adherence to the initiatives. [Shorthand term: Do it or else.]

Each of these forms of influence has a place. Often a leader will employ one, two, three, or four. For example, during a reorganization, the CEO will make the business case (information) but then quickly move to the why and wherefore (reason). Ultimately, she may appeal to the heart (emotion) and actively ask for everyone's support (participation). In extreme cases, insist on strict adherence or else (coercion). Influence then can take many styles. For the leader, however, it is important to keep focused on the outcome as well as how the outcome is achieved.

The View from the Middle

Those in the middle of the management food chain need to be vigilant to what is happening within their own organization, above and below them. They need to keep an ear to the ground. To be fair, it is not easy to do. The calendars of middle managers are chock full of meetings, plane rides, dinners, lunches, and even breakfasts. It takes real effort to break the schedule deadlock and meet with front-line folks, especially when those above you are asking to see you. Here are some suggestions.

BE SEEN

Managers who "fly the desk" become skilled at maneuvering around roadblocks, but the trouble is, their vision is more tunnel-like than leader-like. By taking time to walk the halls, eat in the cafeteria, or join employee social gatherings, they pick up the pulse of the organization. Better yet, they are available for people to see and speak to. Employees will know their managers are more likely to share ideas with them. Google, the search engine giant, takes this one step further: It provides meals for its employees. In this way, as Eric Schmidt, the CEO puts it, the company build "passion" for the business and support for new ideas.[11]

Be Curious

It is not enough to just mingle, you have to ask people what's going on. Find out what people are working on and how they are doing it. Ask what customers are thinking and how they are reacting to your products and services. Solicit ideas and give feedback. Howard Lester, CEO of Williams Sonoma, insists that his top people spend time in the stores. "We say all the answers are in the stores or in the care centers where we talk to our direct customers."[12] The curious manager is the one who is attuned to her organization.

Celebrate Ideas

Many companies that think they are innovative really are not. New product introductions are not innovative per se; they are often pro forma. By contrast, innovative companies are those that cherish the input of their people and act as if they matter. How? They recognize people for their achievements with rewards that are tangible — incentives and bonuses. Furthermore, they post names of achievers in the hall or on the website. They have employee celebration days that thank employees for their good ideas. Such practices are not reserved for just high-tech companies but all kinds of companies involved in manufacturing, logistics, healthcare, and service.

The View Looking Up

A while back I received an email from a young man requesting my advice on gaining the ear of senior management for his ideas. As he explained in his email, he was a good communicator in social situations but wondered how he could become a better communicator in upward business communications. He seemed to be doing all the right things, working hard, showing willingness to make a positive contribution, and generating ideas that complement strategic goals. The situation facing this young man — that he was not connecting his ideas to the needs above him — is not unique; sadly, it happens all too often. The consequences of failing to be heard can be costly. So let's show how a manager who needs to sell an idea upward can do it.

KNOW THE REAL SITUATION

Bono, as we have seen, knows that he can reach policy decision makers by presenting the facts. It is essential, therefore, to be totally accurate. A misstated or misused fact will give those against you the ammunition they need to destroy your argument and perhaps you in the process. The same holds for those of us in the corporate world. If you a proposing a new product, process, or service, know how it will benefit the company financially (improving the bottom line) as well as performance wise (improving work conditions). Be certain to include the competition in your analysis. Companies, like ideas, do not operate within a vacuum.

DEVELOP YOUR STORY

Before you pitch, you had better be prepared. Fact checking is only step one. Develop an argument, both written and oral, that presents your ideas in terms of the business case. You can be artful in your formal presentation: tell a story, paint a picture, or even develop a skit. What you want to do is make your idea come alive, not simply in terms of business metrics but in what idea will mean to people — employees, customers, and shareholders. Also, make certain you craft a 30-second elevator speech that captures the essence of your idea. People will hear about what you are doing and want to know what's going on.

BUILD A COALITION AROUND YOUR IDEAS

There is nobility in the lone crusader championing an idea. But reality is that isolated crusaders can be easily crushed; you need allies. Start spreading the word among your peers. Win them over to your side with the strength of your argument as well as an offer to do something positive for them, e.g., support one of their ideas. Coalition building is more art than exercise but the more you do it, often the better at it you will become. And if you are looking to move up within the organization, knowing how to bring people together is essential to leadership success. *[More on this topic in the next chapter.]*

LEVERAGE YOUR CUSTOMERS

As a middle manager, our greatest allies may be the people to whom you sell and serve — your customers. If you frame your idea in terms of what they are asking for, you will stand a better chance of being heard. By adopting your customers' point of view, you become their advocate. You champion what you think and hope is good for them. Such an argument applies to internal customers, too. Scott Cook, founder of Intuit, says the idea of Quick-Books did not come from a "big fancy R&D lab." To the contrary, QuickBooks "came out of us being closer to understanding the customer and the prospect better than anyone else."[13]

KEEP PUSHING

Too many good ideas are forfeited the first time someone says no. That is a shame because often the first no is a good indication that you might be onto something good. Find out why the idea was rejected. Perhaps you need to make an adjustment in the idea, add some new element, or combine it with another idea from someone else. You will never know unless you persist in your ideas. If you keep pushing, sooner or later your tenacity will win you some points, as long as you are earnest, courteous, and in keeping with corporate strategies. In other words, your idea might not fly, but your career will. Organizations need leaders who do not buckle at the first obstacle; adversity is a marvelous teacher.

Relate to People as People

If you scan advertisements for middle management positions, you will encounter ads asking for executives with "excellent communication, influencing, and relationship-building skills." This phrase summarizes a key behavior that leaders who want to lead up must possess: an ability to relate and influence others. While these ads itemize competencies related to the function (marketing, operations, finance), most ads also emphasize the need for managers who can work well with others. Management relates to job competency; leadership relates to inspiring people. That is the salient point of any senior leadership position.

Executives who can read a balance sheet, crunch numbers, or develop net debt equity strategies are not hard to find. Executives who can communicate, influence, and build relationships are less common and therefore in high demand. Part of these abilities are rooted in emotional intelligence; as you may recall from the previous chapter, EQ is the ability to get along with others. Good emotional intelligence is essential to good communication, especially when it comes to influencing others. You need to connect with people as people before you can deliver a point of view, offer reasons for following that point of view, and ask them to support you. So consider:

EMPHASIZE THE HUMAN SIDE

Management is a discipline focused on administration to obtain intended results. As important as management is, it cannot survive without people. For many organizations the "people are our most valuable resource" is a cliché because senior management acts only on the bottom line, not the people line. By contrast, successful organizations thrive because they do put people in positions where they can succeed. Managers walk the talk; they connect with people and thereby spread influence toward personal and corporate goals.

ADOPT AN ALTERNATE POINT OF VIEW

It requires great discipline to look at a situation the way an employee does. Experienced managers may think they know the correct way because they have done it this way so long. In doing so, they cut off any discussion, or worse, they prevent their people from looking at problems or opportunities with fresh eyes. If you want to influence someone, you must first understand him or her. And understanding begins with give-and-take and at least an acknowledgment of alternate approaches.

Sell Your Idea

One reason people stand back from salespeople is because they resist being persuaded. Leaders cannot take that luxury. Like effective salespeople, they must take the time to create the relationship that enables another person to see the benefits of an idea. What works most effectively is the personal approach, e.g., what's in it for me? If a department is being reorganized, the manager must find some way of showing how the reorganization will make things better in terms of time, process, and efficiency. This is not always easy, but it is necessary.

Teach People to Network

Reach across the aisle. While we don't see much of that in the halls of Congress today, once upon a time Democrats and Republicans argued over the issues, but socialized over cocktails, golf, or other political affairs. They related to one another as people. Former Senate Majority Leader Bob Dole was a master at networking with both parties, as was a predecessor in that role, Senator Lyndon B. Johnson. You can network with people who agree with you, as well as those who do not. But you need to connect to both sides on a human level, otherwise you will be known only by your position, not your capabilities.

Show Enthusiasm

Influence is a human dynamic. It is the result of an emotional connection. Nothing electrifies that connection better than some old-fashioned enthusiasm. Think Teddy Roosevelt! The picture of his toothy grin and twinkling eyes convinces you that he loved being in charge. His enthusiasm was irresistible. People want their leaders to be enthusiastic because if they are not, then what's the point of following them?

Present Your Ideas

Influencing others to achieve leadership goals gets to the heart of achieving results. No leader, especially one leading from the middle, can do it alone; she needs the support of others on her team and her organization to succeed. That's why the ability to communicate face to face, or network to network, is so vital to the enterprise. No organization can have enough leaders who know how to connect with employees on a level that taps into their hopes and aspirations. They want to do the job because it is important to them personally. That's leadership influence, and it's in high demand everywhere. An important element in getting your ideas across is how you present them. Sometimes the conversational approach, one on one, is the best. Other times you need to be more formal. As you develop an approach to your presentation, here are things to consider.

TELL THE BENEFITS STORY

The way you connect with your listener is by focusing on what is important to her. Talk about how your idea, be it a product, process, or service, will make life easier, better, and more fulfilling. For example, be specific about improvements. Tell the story but keep it simple and accessible. One method that entrepreneurs seeking venture capital employ is storytelling. In addition to the business plan, they tell a story about how their product or service will make life better for their customers.

GIVE YOUR IDEAS SEX APPEAL

People like to be sold. They will not admit it openly, but so many of us want to be persuaded. They will put up barriers, but if you are compelling, you can overcome them. Therefore, make your ideas sizzle. Talk up how they will put the listener on the leading edge, or make him the envy of his colleagues. Give people reasons to believe in what you are saying. For example, include customer testimonials as a salesperson might do. By lending your idea credibility, along with snap and sparkle, you make it stand out, and you will increase its chances of being accepted.

Create Urgency

Every salesperson will tell you that if you give the customer too much time, not time enough, he will not close the deal. Therefore, you want to talk about the need to act in a timely fashion. Urgency must be implied so that you give people a reason to go for your idea. Do not overstate the timeline, unless the proverbial sky is falling, but let it be known that acceptance of your idea is a wise move.

How you give the presentation depends upon to whom you are presenting. If you are pitching to the board of directors, a formal report may be in order. If you are presenting to colleagues, you may present your ideas orally. Same holds for customers. On the other hand, you can always develop a detailed report tailored to your audience and then give a presentation that is more of a narrative. Tell them a story about how your idea will make life better for them. For example, if you are pitching a new process, talk about what life will be like when the new process is implemented. Talk about the hours they will trim and the dollars they will save. If you are pitching a new product, focus on how the product will improve their lives.

Respect One Another

Not every idea proposed is feasible. It may be too costly, too unwieldy to implement, or not within the scope of business. Employees and managers need to work together on good ideas. They need to understand the other's point of view. It is human nature to think that one's own ideas trump all others, but that's an unrealistic point of view, as onerous as a boss who slams the door, literally or figuratively, on an employee's pet idea. Both need to listen to one another. This, of course, can only occur if employee and manager trust one another; trust cannot be instituted, it must be earned. How? By demonstrating respect for ideas as well as respect for people. Disagreements will, and frankly should, arise, but the disagreements must be focused on the ideas, not those proposing the ideas. Ad hominen attacks are not only nasty, they are disruptive to performance because they distract from the real business at hand — learning from one another.

Dr. Susan Desmond-Hellman realized that her skills as an oncologist could help hundreds of cancer patients; as a researcher, she could help many thousands more. And that is the route she took, becoming president of product development at Genentech, now part of the Swiss drugmaker, Roche. As the *Wall Street Journal* reported in 2004, Dr. Desmond-Hellmann helped to shift the biotech's focus to cancer treatment. Working in partnership with colleagues, Dr. Desmond-Hellmann helped Genentech bring three cancer drugs to market in less than ten years.[14]

Your ability to sell your ideas really comes down to how you sell yourself. When people trust you, they will trust your ideas. Therefore, you must be motivated to find ways to demonstrate you can do what you say you will do. How you handle responsibility and manifest accountability says a great deal about your personal leadership skills. When you are credible, people will want to listen to what you have to say.

Influence Across Borders

One of the great and seemingly lasting changes in the management landscape is the move to flatter organizations. This trend directly affects managers in the middle. Hierarchies have been squished into more linear organizations where there are fewer at the top and many more in the middle on one level. The U.S. Marines have used this model for eons; the officer corps is quite small; the bulk of the force is comprised of noncommissioned officers and front-line ranks. In the private sector, some organizations are more horizontal — professional service firms and advertising agencies, for example. There are the partners who manage, but the consulting and creative work is done by consultants and creatives who are within the same management band. Their rewards come from the quality of their ideas and the application of those ideas to specific client issues and problems. And that's the point of linear organizations — more teamwork, more autonomy, and more innovation. The downside is that unless the organization is well managed, it devolves into chaos. You need strong-minded managers who can lead, if not by rank, then by the power of influence.

Influencing across borders, that is, outside of your function or department, is both an art and a practice. The art comes from an ability to read the situation and then understand the people in it. The practice comes from the experience of having done it as well as the knowledge of which levers to pull in order to get things done. And it is an art and practice that those leading up need to master.

The medical community is a prime example of influence without hierarchy. Physicians adopt best practices of other physicians because those physicians are known, respected, and achieve good outcomes. Often, those pioneering the research or the therapies are in the universities, but not always. The new methodologies take hold in private practice, where most patients receive care. Other than seniority, there is little hierarchy per se in private practice. Good therapies spread because physicians document their results, present at conferences, and spread the word informally among their networks. Seniority is a factor, but because it is earned; just because a physician has been practicing a while does not automatically confer respect; she must have a good track record of success as well as an ability to connect with fellow physicians. In other words, she has influence.

Influencing across borders in organizations is both easier and trickier. It is easier because it is often sanctioned from on high. For example, many companies are adopting a lean philosophy as it applies not only to manufacturing, but also to operations — finance, marketing, purchasing, etc. Disciplines of lean must teach its principles to people in different departments and in large corporations' entire divisions or companies. That's where it becomes tricky because it falls to the disciple to convince people that lean is better and why. Lean is only one of many initiatives (others include Six Sigma and Balanced Scorecard) that rely more on the influencer than on a dictate from on high. Such influence requires a deft blend of insight and skills. Here are some suggestions.

STUDY THE SITUATION

You know the old saying, "before you can know another man, you must walk a mile in his shoes." This adage has great bearing on those who must persuade. You need to know the situation before you enter it. Sizing up the situation requires knowing the people in it. Take care to identify who may support you as well as who may disagree with you. Learn what came before you; for example, has this department ever tried to adopt a process change? If so, what worked and what didn't. Ask questions to find out what you need to know. So often change fails because it is imposed rather than adopted. Adoption requires consent; influencers work for consent.

BE AVAILABLE TO HELP

Change is burdensome, and even when people say yes, they need nudging. Successful people of influence make themselves available. They don't cut and run; they stay in the loop, offering advice and counsel as well as continuing to teach. They create fellow teachers; in fact, this is the methodology of Six Sigma. Master teachers are black belts, and they travel through the organization spreading their lessons, in turn educating green belts, those on the first rung of the Six Sigma mastery process.

Tell Stories

We relate to ideas on a personal level. While data points may justify a decision, they seldom excite us. What captures our hearts is the personal. People want to experience the WIFM (what's in it for me). The best way to demonstrate it is through story. Influencers can tell success stories about people who have adopted the initiative and succeeded. The stories must be real, that is, present the challenges as well as the outcomes.

Walk Humbly

The last thing a person of influence should be is arrogant. If you project a know-it-all, "been there done that" attitude, then people will shut you down before you finish your first meeting. Keep in mind that few of us want to change; we like things to stay the same for us, but change for other people. So if you can convince people that things will be better but do it in a way that projects humility, you will succeed. Think of the Dalai Lama; as the spiritual leader of Tibet, he lives in exile. His only means of influence is the power of his example, so he leads a humble and prayerful life that demonstrates his compassion for all who suffer as well as those in his homeland.

Make Your Case

For anyone leading from the middle, influence is an active process. It requires commitment to the vision, the discipline to implement, and the patience to practice it continually. There are many models of influence, that is, action steps you can follow to begin the process of persuading and influencing others. Here is one that emphasizes the business case — that is, what we must do to accomplish our goals. This model draws upon many time-tested action steps that experienced persuaders and influences have used for generations. As you employ these steps, you may find yourself going back and forth between steps, even going back to the beginning and leaping ahead. The reason is that most work environments are changing, and leaders need to be adept enough to recognize the shifting sands as well as adaptable enough to do what is necessary to keep the case of influence moving forward.

SCAN THE HORIZON

Look for what is happening in the organization. For example, is the organization going through a form of transition, such as reorganization or pending merger? Influencers should determine the external challenges facing the organization in terms of competitors, global and local trends, and general health of the industry. It is essential to diagnose organizational health; that is, are people engaged in their work, do they trust their managers, and do they enjoy belonging to the organization? The answers to questions such as these will enable you to shape your influence argument.

IDENTIFY THE PLUSES AND MINUSES

Discover those factors that positively affect your degree of influence as well as those that may detract from it. Those factors may be economic, political, or people. For example, if you are championing reorganization and the organizational climate is toxic, few people are going to want to listen to what you have to say, let alone be persuaded by your argument. Nonetheless, you should do some organizational mapping to identify people who will support you as well as those who may oppose you. Opposition will occur in the healthiest organizations; in fact, good influencers even welcome opposition because it gives them the opportunity to develop and make their case in a more realistic fashion.

ARGUE THE VALUE PROPOSITION

Focus on what will improve the organization. Emphasize that your argument is based on empirical data. Demonstrate the value that your case adds to the organization. In fact, if you are not adding value, you really have no business making a case. The great philosopher of continuous improvement known as kaizen,

Masaaki Imai, defines *gemba* (Japanese for "real place") as "the place where the products or services are formed." According to Imai, "management must maintain close contact with the realities of *gemba* in order to solve whatever problems arise there."[15] That is sound advice for anyone developing a business case. Get to the core of your argument and demonstrate how it will make things better for customers, employees, and the company. Most important, avoid personality contests. That's a losing proposition. By focusing on value, you will take your case to a higher level where it belongs.

MAKE THE BUSINESS CASE

Facts make persuasion easier. Demonstrate the features and benefits of your initiative. Relate those facts to organizational improvement; that is, we can do things faster, better, easier, and less expensively. Make certain to link the business case to the personal. Explain why it will be better for individuals. Show ways that your ideas will benefit them. This is not always possible. In fact, your good idea may mean that certain individuals will lose some of their independence or decision-making authority. If this is the case, find ways to maximize their autonomy in other areas. Lean, for example, requires a high degree of thinking, decision making, and autonomy on a local level.

OVERCOME OBSTACLES

Not everything will fall your way. You could be sailing along smoothly with seemingly no opposition, when suddenly, the roof falls in. This may happen due to the emergence of a new competitor, the sudden appointment of a new senior executive, or simply changing business trends. Be prepared to revise your argument and account for new factors. You may also anticipate obstacles, too. Develop your case for overcoming them. The more robust your case, as well as the more resilience you show, the better chance you have of overcoming what comes your way.

Go for the Heart

As much as you base your argument on fact, you make it real. Few of us outside of the boardroom get excited about strategic propositions; we get enthused about making a positive difference for ourselves, our team, and our company. Talk up the potential benefits for individuals. Talk about how individuals will benefit from your case. This is essential for arguing initiatives across borders. People want to feel that you have their best interests at heart. Of course, this is not always possible, but do what you can to frame arguments in individual terms, that is, what's in it for me in terms of doing my job and my opportunities for advancement and growth. You strive always for commitment versus compliance. When you capture people's hearts as well as their heads, commitment is more attainable as well as actionable.

Create Win-Wins

You want to win your argument. You also want people to embrace your cause, but you want to make certain that people will support you, not simply go through the motions. One way is to make certain that all parties, including those whose objections you overcame, feel they are winning, too. For example, if you have won permission for launching a new product over the objection of someone more senior or who proposed something similar, have a conversation with that person. Invite her to contribute ideas or resources. You may even propose she join your team. Magnanimity in victory will win you favors and maybe even some friends. But you are not acting simply to be a nice person, you are acting to create ownership, a factor that engenders commitment, perhaps not immediately, but in time certainly.

Few cases of influence are exactly the same because no two people are exactly the same. You will also find yourself repeating this model again and again. For example, in one instance, you may be in the scan stage; in another instance, you may be in the overcome stage. That is to be expected and shows that you are active in persuading others to your cause. If this model does not wholly work for you, find another, or develop your own. The important thing is that you leverage your leadership to bring others together around a common cause.

Deal with the Limits of Influence

Of course there will be times when the art of influence meets the wall of resistance in the form of a manager who will simply say no. And that manager, typically by virtue of seniority and acquired skill in saying no, will prevail. Then influence wanes, and unless the initiative comes in the form of a direct order from a senior manager, nothing will change. The sad part is that many times people doing the work, often under the manager, want to adopt the new initiative. They see its virtues and are frustrated when it is not adopted. True enough, there are many stories of employees doing what they think is best, despite their manager's reluctance.

Influencing across borders is never easy. It can be a long and tedious practice. It requires great patience for several reasons. One, influencers must learn to repeat themselves again and again. Skilled influencers know that what they are teaching is new, so they try to make it sound fresh and lively. Two, influencers put up with resistance again and again; that is wearying. Just once, they say to themselves, they'd love to work with a team whose managers and employees say yes, yes, yes. Seldom does that occur, but even if it did, such adoption may not be best. Why? Because if an initiative, be it lean or Six Sigma, is not discussed, debated, and even fought over internally, it becomes just one of many ideas that can be easily discarded. The good fight that is won indicates that the influencer has indeed influenced positively; people have adopted the idea and, most important, made it their own.

Advocate

A few years ago a large manufacturing company was seeking to reinvigorate its brand image. It was decided that the company should enlist the support of employees and its franchise network to help plead that case. Both constituents could advocate in their unique ways, as people with vested interests but also as representatives of the communities in which they lived. It was a great idea, but sadly, it never gained traction. The reason was that the initiative became lost in the mix of other pressing issues; as a result, the company lost an opportunity to elevate its public profile in a positive way.

By contrast, Wal-Mart learned how to advocate on its own behalf. For years, the giant retailer prided itself on flying under the radar, but when it became the largest retailer in the world, stealth was impossible. In response to perceived negative publicity about destroying small mom-and-pop retail operations and genuine negative reaction over sexual discrimination lawsuits, Wal-Mart became more aggressive in its public relations as well as in its advertising. As reported in the *New York Times*, Lee Scott, then CEO of Wal-Mart, became vocal about articulating his company's point of view on providing employee healthcare, something that the company does not offer most of its employees, many of whom are part-timers. The company has also enlisted the support of bloggers in their public relations efforts. Rather than dismissing public criticism, Wal-Mart confronted it, and then sought to advocate its point of view.[16]

Advocacy is a leadership proposition. It involves standing up for what you believe in, which those who lead up are good at doing. If individuals or organizations never take a stand, then it means they have little to offer. For example, if you launch a product but fail to support it with advertising or public relations, then you are demonstrating you have little faith in it. Likewise, if a CEO launches an initiative inside the company, perhaps a reorganization or a renewed commitment to quality, but fails to support it with communications to employees, then that initiative, no matter how important, is dead on arrival.

Advocacy is a form of communicatons, and as such it requires great energy and commitment. And if the issue is important enough, you may wish to enlist the support of employees and key stakeholders, that is, suppliers and board members. That is what effective managers who lead from the middle are accustomed to doing. Before you can advocate, however, you must ensure understanding of issues as well as create proper platforms for action. Here are some suggestions:

INFORM

Provide information about the issues and how they affect the organization. If legislation is involved, talk about the impact the law will have on the business. If pushing for reform is involved, discuss the expected benefits. Translate the benefits into personal terms, that is, how the issue affects individuals. Does the legislation make work safer or threaten job security? Does the reform initiative mean cleaner air for everyone? Whatever the issue, make it real. The military does a good job of communicating its point of view on issues related to the local communities in which it has bases. Issues discussed involve everything from employment and noise control to economic impact on local businesses. Such issues are always top of mind when base closures are debated.

TEACH

Once people know the issues and how they affect them, you want to teach them how to articulate their point of view. Some may wish to speak only to friends; others may be excited to write a letter to the editor or even speak at a community meeting. Encourage them to speak from the heart and put the case into their own words. Otherwise, they will sound like automatons, and that will do more harm than good. Hold classes in how to articulate the advocacy case. One pharmaceutical company has adopted this approach, and in so doing, enabled employees who wished to lobby issues to do so. The teaching phase is also good experience for those who must articulate the case. Former chairman of the Federal Reserve, Alan Greenspan, once said, "If you cannot persuade your colleagues of the correctness of your decision, it is probably worthwhile to re-think your own." That is, you better know your stuff.

Prepare

If you expect employees to advocate on your behalf, you must pre-pare for them for adversity. Give them instruction as well as materi-als on how to handle objections. Again, speaking from the heart is better than speaking from a briefing book. Encourage them to trans-late their personal commitment into organizational action. The civil rights movements of the 1960s took great effort to teach nonviolence as well as to teach participants how to react when being clubbed or gassed by hostile police forces. Fortunately, few corporate advocates will ever face anything so dire, but the lesson of preparation holds. Know the objections you may face and prepare for them.

Stick to Your Knitting

When you ask employees to advocate for something, especially for outside the organization, you must do so carefully. Keep in mind the chief function of your organization is to either provide a prod-uct, a service, or a combination thereof. That is what you do. If everyone is off advocating, be it a request for tax abatement or a testimony on product quality, a question may arise: Who's mind-ing the store? Therefore, when advocating, make certain it is fo-cused on business issues. When advocating is not handled by a senior leader or public relations professional, participation should be discreet and minimized. Also, never pressure an employee to participate. Such pressure will backfire. Advocacy must come from the heart, if the person does not feel compelled by the issue, or is reluctant for other reasons, back off. Your case will be better for it.

Caring enough about the issues that face the organization to voice an opinion is a demonstration of a commitment to values. When done in ways that present a point of view that promotes the livelihood of stakeholders as well as commitment to corporate citizenship, it is very much a leadership proposition. At times, the point of view will be unpopular with certain constituents, but that is always the challenge of leadership, making tough choices in tough times. Leaders, especially those in middle management, need to be strong when arguing their case. "If you have an important point to make, don't try to be subtle or clever," said Winston Churchill. "Use a pile driver. Hit the point once. Then come back and hit it again. Then a third time — a tremendous whack!" Advocacy is not for the faint of heart, but it is something that leaders who lead up must embrace.[17]

What You Need to Do to Break Down the Doors

The team needs someone who is not afraid to try new things in order to achieve intended results. This requires someone with an ability to collaborate with people who have no interest in his or her ideas. Therefore, you have to learn to lead when you have no authority to do so. You must prove that you know your stuff. You must use your wits and your influence to succeed. And by doing so you create opportunities for people to listen to what you have to say and give you a chance to prove your case.

To break down the doors, you will need to:
- Learn the principles of influence.
- Balance the need to look out with the need to lead up.
- Keep the needs of your people foremost.
- Overcome obstacles.
- Turn influence into leadership.

WORKING THE SYSTEM

*Moderation in temper is always a virtue, but moderation
in principle is always a vice.*

THOMAS PAINE, *RIGHTS OF MAN*[1]

Watching her walk through the village smiling and nodding to passers-by is an indication of the respect in which she is held. Her demeanor is one of serenity, but her presence is one of authority. She is Rohima, a volunteer health worker, laboring among the village folk of Bangladesh. That she does what she does today, diagnosing simple ailments, delivering medicines, and tending to the sick, is a testament to her own inner fortitude. Forced into a marriage as a child bride, she was thrown out onto the street after her husband was killed in the Bangladeshi war for independence, leaving her destitute and pregnant. She turned to growing vegetables and begging as a means to survive. Eventually, she found a program that was recruiting women to become volunteer healthcare workers. She gladly signed up, became trained in simple medicine, and took to her calling.

Today she is a village elder as well as something of an entrepreneur. Taking advantage of a micro-loan program, she owns a small pharmacy that her son, now a young man, helps her to run. It is gratifying to watch Rohima speak to her patients sometimes as wise matriarch, advising a young woman to get on birth control, or as a skilled practitioner showing a man how to spit into a cup for a tuberculosis test, and last for this same man, as a nurse, kindly and gently stroking him as she informed him at his TB test was positive, but offering the comforting advice that she had medicine that would help him get well.

Much of what Rohima has been able to accomplish is due the effort of Fazle Hasan Abed. Trained as an engineer, Abed is among the educated elite of Bangladesh. After the cyclone of 1971 and the war of 1972, he turned his attention and his skills toward helping his own populace. He founded the Bangladeshi Rural Advancement Committee (BRAC). Its first task was to tackle the seemingly intractable program of infant death due to diarrhea. The solution was simple, an oral rehydration solution made from sugar, salt, and water — something that virtually everyone in the rural areas had access to. Persuasion was another matter. "That involved going to every household in rural Bangladesh — 13 million households," says Abed. "And it took 10 years." The results were worth it; the oral rehydration program reduced the death rate for children and adults by 70 percent.

That gave Abed and BRAC credibility that it has leveraged to the advantage of the rural populace of Bangladesh. BRAC has created micro-finance organizations that have enabled women like Rohima to run their own businesses. As of 2006, BRAC had dispensed over one billion dollars in such micro-loans. BRAC also runs its own enterprises, which in turn provide for 80 percent of operating costs. The money helps to fund many other health initiatives, including one for the fight against tuberculosis.

Abed himself, like Rohima, has the common touch. Watching him visit one of the more than 68,000 villages where BRAC programs are active is to witness a man whose compassion is evident in his radiant smile. You can see the joy in his eyes as he speaks and joshes with women volunteers. His presence virtually glows, however, when he listens to school children in a BRAC program read aloud in English. Education, Abed knows, is the key to unlocking the figurative chains that bind these children and their parents to a life of grinding poverty. Rohima, a common woman by birth, and Abed, a man born to comparative privilege, both demonstrate very difference kinds of presence that is focused on achieving good for their respective communities. Perhaps Rohima put her task, and Abed's, in the best light with his quote: "When I walk through my village, people stop me all the time. They seek my advice, ask me how I'm doing. I see how things are improving, and I feel very happy."[2]

What Rohima Teaches Us About Leading Up:

- Have a goal by which you set your internal compass.
- Overcome obstacles by enlisting the trust of those above you.
- Do not let obstacles stand in the way of achieving your goal.

■ ■ ■

Rohima, a community organizer of humble origin, had the gumption to challenge the status quo and in the process achieved something unique. That is the challenge that managers who wish to lead up within their organizations face. Resisters will outnumber supporters, but the manager who looks to make the positive difference will triumph. This difference will begin with a challenge to assumptions. The willingness to rethink options leads to the creation of new possibilities. Those who are in the middle of the hierarchy are well poised to challenge assumptions because they see the effect of assumptions that do not work. At the same time, those in the middle find it uncomfortable to go against those in authority. That is a natural feeling, so what the manager who seeks to lead up needs to do is find ways to challenge assumptions without challenging the individual above him or her. That is, frame the challenge over ideas not personalities.

Establish Meaningful Priorities

Challenges begin with priorities, that is, what needs doing. As straightforward as setting priorities may be, the concept of prioritization becomes muddled. How? At the end of the year, the dutiful manager plans out his year and sketches the objectives. The plan is blessed by the boss and implemented first of the year. Long about February, or maybe even the last week of January, the first crisis of the year hits — a system fails, a software patch becomes unglued, or a competitor introduces a new product. All the objectives so carefully planned and neatly articulated get sidetracked, likely never to be tracked the remainder of the year as the manager and his team lurch from problem to problem. Crises cannot be predicted, but they can be planned for, subsequently managed, and even worked into the normal job flow with enough forethought and yes, you guessed it — prioritization! Here are two ways to communicate priorities to those you seek to lead, including your boss.

TELL PEOPLE WHAT THEY NEED TO KNOW

Knowledge is power. Unlike information, which can be withheld, knowledge resides within the capability of people to do their jobs. Sharing knowledge is paramount; effective teams are those where managers and members share what they know and do in order to get things done the right way. Such cooperation has another benefit — it evokes trust. Trust is integral to prioritization for one of many reasons; let me offer two. One, trust enables the manager to set objectives and then change them without people pushing back too hard. They may complain, but they understand their manager is only responding to change, not acting on personal whim. Two, trust gives managers the flexibility to ask their people for more in terms of hours and commitment in tough times because they know she will find a way to recognize (or maybe even reward) their extra effort at some later date.

RADIATE CALM

Nothing reassures a team more than a confident manager. One such example is film director Clint Eastwood. The tough guy stance he plays in his movies is nowhere to be found on the set. Instead, actors find a director who understands how to put them at ease. While stories are legion about movie sets where the real *sturm und drang* is behind the camera, Eastwood's sets are famous for operating with cool efficiency that puts the cast, crew, and penny-pinching studio bosses at ease. The calm that Eastwood and company radiate is not by chance; it emerges from years of working together as well as meticulous prioritization that takes into account the crises that can bedevil a movie set — weather, scheduling, and accidents.[3]

Understand the Change Factor

As prepared as you are, things are always subject to change. In his book, *Homicide: A Year on the Killing Streets*, author David Simon (a subsequently a successful television writer/producer of hit shows like *The Wire*) profiles a group of Baltimore detectives working, as the eponymous title indicates, homicides. The detectives work in teams and largely at the pace the investigation would permit: dogged, determined, disciplined. There was one exception — the "red ball," so named for the red dot ascribed beside the victim's name on the unit's white board. The term refers to high priority alert, as in all available hands must work the case. Red balls are reserved for high-profile crimes of a particularly heinous nature. In the adaptation of the book as an award-winning police drama, red ball cases accelerated the dramatic pace in contrast to the otherwise detached and even laconic nature of police investigations. Most often red balls produced results; murderers were caught, but not always. Even so, after a time, the pace of the investigation slackened, and most detectives went back to their own cases.[4]

Red balls are not reserved for police departments. Middle managers face their own hot issues on a daily basis. But all too often, unlike their counterparts on the crime beat, the pace never slackens; red balls burn and sizzle day after day for months on end. The result, sadly, is that work gets done but at a cost that is way too high — on-the-job burnout. It therefore falls to a manager to prioritize the tasks and communicate their respective levels of urgency.

While prioritization is fundamental to effective management, no amount of task analysis and planning can account for the change factor. As Dwight Eisenhower once quipped, "Plans are nothing; planning is everything." Whether it is a macro change affecting market conditions and product trends or a micro change affecting corporate policies and people, the concept of flexibility must be accommodated. If managers cannot respond to change, then prioritization becomes no more realistic than a Soviet politburo Five Year Plan — meaningless!

Middle managers who prioritize and communicate those priorities will often get things done within deadlines and close to budget. Even more remarkably, managers will accomplish this without alienating their people. In fact, they will accomplish their goals *because of* their people. Manager and employees will have become, to risk using another buzz phrase, a "highly performing team." Prioritization is essential, but it can only truly work when people know and understand one another because they have communicated clearly and openly with one another. Not an easy task, but a laudable aspiration that just might help alleviate the heat of the next crisis.

Manage the Mind

One of the great unintended consequences of management is that managers seem to lose the ability to do anything for themselves. The skills that got them promoted have atrophied from lack of use. This phenomenon was illustrated to me some years back by a friend who was then working as a business broker identifying and qualifying people who wanted to buy small businesses. Many of the initial takers were executives who had been laid off from a senior level position and were looking to start fresh. It was a noble thought, but these men (yes, it was mostly male then) were about as qualified to run a small business, be it a printer, a shipper, or distributor, as they were to pilot a space ship to Mars. Simple tasks like paying billings, hiring new help, or even making photocopies seemed beyond them. The reason: They had not done such things, because while working for a large organization so much was done for them. As a result, they became as noblemen at Versailles — utterly useless.

While managers need to stop doing day-to-day tasks, they should never surrender their skill set. Again, this was illustrated by another colleague who was working as an executive coach. The selection process he had to undergo was particularly onerous — not because of the coachee client but because of the client's company. The people in human resources acted as if the executive was wholly incapable of making the right selection. Such behavior is not confined to coaching; I have seen it again and again in issues related to everything from strategy to communications. One reason why so many companies stumbled and fell in this last recession is that they had outsourced key decisions to strategic consulting firms and seemed incapable of making decisions themselves. This not only doomed senior managers who should have been managing in the first place, but it also gave the consulting business a black eye, which in some cases was certainly deserved.

Keeping a hand in the doing is essential to management, especially those leading up. Yet it can have a downside. Too much doing will be interpreted as micro-management; too little doing will be regarded as loafing. Striking the right balance is essential, and here are some suggestions for keeping your skills sharp while maintaining your leadership poise.

MAKE YOURSELF AVAILABLE

Perceptions to the contrary, some employees do welcome input from the boss for several reasons. One, it assures them that they are on the right track; two, it provides face time so that boss and employee can get to know each other's working styles. Just as too much physical contact in basketball will get you whistled for a foul, too much "management contact" will squash initiative and turn employees into dependents. Give your people room to breathe.

MAKE THE BIG DECISIONS

Decision making drives the enterprise. It is what organizations are supposed to do. As a matter of survival, you want to have managers at all levels making decisions; otherwise, organizations become paralyzed. But when the entire enterprise is at stake, then you want the big guy or gal to weigh in. The bigger the title, the bigger the decisions. Keeping the mind flexed for such decisions is a matter of knowing your people, mastering key details, understanding the strategy, and focusing on the outcome. That's a role for senior leadership.

DIVE INTO A PROJECT

One way to get your mind engaged is to plunge into a special project. Take the lead and bring others into process. Keep in mind, you have other management responsibilities. Some you may delegate to others, others you cannot. But getting involved day to day with a new product launch, customer service enhancement, or process re-engineering may invigorate the brain cells and keep your mind nimble. Bill Gates serves as a model for this. Now, as Microsoft's chief visionary, he delves into projects that he feels are important to the company and where his engagement can make a positive difference.

THINK LIKE A GUIDE

That phrase (like leading up) comes from Michael Useem, a professor at Wharton School as well as an experienced mountain climber. Mike has led MBA teams from his school as well as corporate executives on climbs to high points throughout the world. "Thinking like a guide," as he writes in *Upward Bound*, is for "the ability to see ahead or to see the whole." It has become a way of doing that has helped him not only shepherd a team through difficulty but also to be watchful for signs of climbers in danger of succumbing to the effects of thin air at high altitude. When you think like a guide, you balance team and individual to find the right blend of achievement over undue stress. It is a mantra that anyone in a position of leadership is wise to follow.[5]

Know That No One Likes Change

Middle managers leading up sometimes experience the feeling of being loneliest person on the planet. You find yourself standing at the front of the room giving a presentation on a new process or methodology. Your job is to convince the people in that room to adopt this new idea. Some are senior in rank to you, others at your level, and one or two junior to you. From the looks on their faces, you know they care very little about what you are saying. To them, you are just another face who's rolling through their world stirring up change for the sake of change. Senior leadership may have blessed this idea and want it put into action right away, but based on the stone-faced looks you are receiving (as well as the inertia in the ranks you can measure), this initiative has about as much opportunity of being accepted as a Martian on Venus. More proverbially, you are the modern equivalent of a door-to-door salesman. People would slam the door in your face if they could, but you're already inside the room.

Being a change agent is not easy. There is a body of literature that rhapsodizes about the dignity and virtue of being a change agent. There is nobility in carrying the torch for change, of being the one at the tip of the spear leading the charge. But let's face it, those who write that kind of stuff have seldom been burned nor run through. Often they are consultants advising on change. [This is a charge to which this consultant can plead guilty.] But what can you do if you are on the ground and you are challenged to persuade a group to embrace change?

MAKE IT SIMPLE

Executives at the top of the house like to dream, or at least, speak in grandiose terms. That's good. They are also fond speaking in terms that only a strategist could love. That's bad. Change agents must make it simple. Avoid jargon. Use everyday language that anyone can understand.

MAKE PEOPLE COMFORTABLE

When you present to a team, put people at ease. Keep your prepared presentation to a minimum. At the outset invite people to ask you questions. Make certain people know that there is no such thing as a dumb question. Give an example of a simple question that indicates you are serious about what you mean. If you are talking about Six Sigma, define what the term means, that is, 3 errors per 100,000. That kind of dialogue will indicate that you will entertain questions no matter how simple they may seem. After all, it's the simple questions that can provoke the greatest insights.

BE SPECIFIC

One of the criticisms often hurled at senior leaders is that their directives are too vague and abstract. As a result of this lack of clarity, employees do not know what they are supposed to do, so they end up churning instead of changing. Good change agents talk about specific action steps that people must to do to make change real. Best of all, they work with teams to quantify change in terms of roles, responsibilities, and tasks. Specificity, particularly when coupled with active participation, makes change tangible and therefore more likely to be implemented.

GIVE PEOPLE THE BUY-IN

It is human nature to want to be invited to contribute, not ordered. Of course, in the real world, managers tell people what to do all the time. That's fine, but once in a while, make it a habit of asking people. When you ask, you open the door to dialogue. More important, you allow people an opportunity to voice an opinion; push back some. Rather than resist that reaction, provoke it so that you can have a conversation. You may not persuade the other person totally, but you will have allowed him a voice in the process. That will go a long way toward acceptance.

MAKE YOURSELF THE BUTT OF THE JOKE

Humor is the great leveler; it defuses tension because it underscores humanity between speaker and listener, persuader and skeptic, change agent and resister. For example, if you are asked to persuade a group of the virtues of some new process, talk about your own initial resistance, either to this initiative or some other one. Joke about how much easier it is for others to change than for yourself to change. That kind of honesty even in jest makes the change agent more likable as well as more credible.

ADD A LITTLE DRAMA

People like to feel part of something greater than themselves. Winston Churchill, as philosopher Isaiah Berlin once observed, made the British people feel as if they were players in a great "epic" of history during the World War II; their contributions and sacrifices were vital to the war effort. Change agents, too, can make people feel important by dramatizing what they do; make their contributions in adopting change vital to the transformation that will transform the organization.[6]

Limit Yourself

Part of effecting change is knowing your own limits. When Rudy Tomjanovich stepped down as head coach of the Los Angeles Lakers in February 2004, he made headlines. The resignation of a coach in mid-season is always news, but Rudy T.'s departure was something a little different. As far as we know, he was not being forced out; he was forcing himself out. He said he was becoming too absorbed in his job, and it was affecting his health. Tomjanovich is a battler; he overcame a devastating injury as a player when he was slugged in the face (an act that inspired a book by John Feinstein), recovered from alcoholism, and survived a bout of bladder cancer. In other words, Tomjanovich recognized his limits and stepped aside. Bravo! His example is a lesson to all managers: Know what you can do and what you cannot do![7]

Management can be brutal. The time pressures are intense, the workload is incessant, and the administration of detail can be draining. Add to that the need to coach your employees, which in reality is what modern management really is, and the wonder is that more managers do not opt out sooner. Tomjanovich could afford it; he was a two-time NBA champion coach of the Houston Rockets and had ample financial resources. But his comments at his departing press conference were revealing; he said he was becoming like an assistant coach, that is, doing their jobs for them. Wisely, Tomjanovich faced up to his leadership responsibility and stopped himself cold. Too many managers fail to do this and end up fracturing their families or ruining their health.

The cry "don't work so hard" falls on deaf ears for two reasons. One, there is much work to do, and in these tough economic times, or even in good times, no good manager wants to slack off. Two, we pride ourselves on working hard; to do anything less is perceived, mostly by ourselves, as a sign of weakness. To the contrary, as Tomjanovich illustrates, moving on in order to move forward is a sign of strength. Not only is it healthy to do for yourself, it is also healthy for the organization. Here are two ways that leaders in the middle can teach this sense of personal limits to others.

Limit the Job

When taking on a job, scope it out. Know the parameters. For example, CIOs must know the parameters of their capacities. Their departmental description will include wording that will encompass every conceivable form of information technology that if read the wrong way could make them responsible for employees' home computers and personal cell phones. To avoid such surprises, define the job and keep to the definition. That means when new assignments arise, as they surely will, you fit them in accordance with their value to the company. Emergencies will occur; handle them. Priorities will shift, so be flexible. You may not accomplish everything, but you will keep things humming and yourself and your people on an even keel.

Hold Yourself Accountable

You might be reading this and saying, this author is nuts; he doesn't know my boss. True enough, but consider that both you and he are accountable to the organization and to each other. So advise him about what you and your people will do. Do not be confrontational; be forthcoming. Discuss all of the variables and then gain agreement on what you will be doing and not doing. In a way, you are coaching your boss; you are demonstrating initiative. But you are making yourself accountable, and by extension, you are linking your boss to your fortunes. This negotiation will not be a one-way ticket to fat city; it may be a side trip to a halfway house; that is, both you and the boss meet each other's needs and in turn the needs of the organization.

But there is a limit to such crises; you can only push so hard. Even those who work in adrenaline-pumping jobs where the challenge fuels the rush — e.g., emergency workers, SWAT team officers, or ER docs to name a few — must take time off. Otherwise, they burn out, and in the process of burning they not only ruin their personal lives, they shred their professional credibility — they become used up hulks of themselves.

The best way to avoid burnout, and to demonstrate that you have what it takes to lead up, is to delegate responsibility and authority to your employees. To some managers this is akin to giving keys to a high-performance vehicle to a 16-year-old. But that's only if they have not prepared their people to take on new responsibilities. If you are always looking over their shoulder, they will always be looking to you, whether it is to requisition a new computer or manage a project across the country. Learn to state your expectations. So push yourself away from their cubicle and walk away. Be available if they need you, but only if it's really necessary.

Learn from Setbacks

Of course, there will be times when you, as one leading from the middle, will fail. Truth be told, most change initiatives do fail. The forces of resistance, either in terms of inertia or hostility, can overwhelm the best of intentions. This is especially true when senior management provides lip service; that is, their lips mouth the right words, but their actions indicate lack of support. In those instances, all you can do is do your job, tell your story, and move forward. Even when the end is in sight, how you carry yourself will mold character as well as prepare you for the next foray into the change landscape. That will be your measure of your potential to assume greater levels of responsibility in the future.

So do not abandon hope. You can use the experience of seeking and working for change to your benefit. You can use it as an opportunity to establish yourself. What matters to those in positions above you is how you conducted yourself during the process. Were you credible? Do you know you stuff? Do you understand us and our business? Your challenge going forward, especially for your future as someone who leads up, is to convince people of your sincerity by your actions and your example. Furthermore, your ability to connect to people as individuals will mark you as a change agent that others will want to follow because they trust you. And there can be no greater accolade to a leader than to be called trustworthy.

What You Need to Do to the Work the System

The team needs someone who can manage the details. A good way to do this is to gain access to the boss's schedule; that will help you determine how the boss spends his or her time. You can then advise your boss on ways to find priorities such as what should be done, what can be done, and what could be done *if* time permits. Leaders also need to make time for others as well as themselves.

To work the system, you will need to:

- Determine priorities in line with your goals. Arrange priorities toward both short- and long-term goals.
- Learn to anticipate, adapt, and embrace change.
- Lead from the front so others can see you.
- Encourage alternative points of view by letting others speak first.
- Learn patience. Resist the urge to complete the work started by others. Give people time and space to do their own work.

PART III

What Can I Do to Help the Leader and the Team Succeed?

ANSWERING THIS QUESTION REQUIRES an ability to match skills and ability to the right thing. Such a leader must be tough and resilient, a teacher of others, and one who leads with authority and presence.

BENDING BUT NOT BREAKING

Fate gave to man the courage of endurance.
LUDWIG VAN BEETHOVEN[1]

The story is told of a young man on the move seeking to make his mark at the 2000 Democratic convention in Los Angeles. He flies out to the city from his hometown of Chicago only to arrive at the convention site to be told that he cannot obtain what he wants: a floor pass. As a state legislator from Illinois, he does not have the chops nor the status to warrant admission to what passes for the power alley of the Democratic Party. Adding insult to injury, he attempts to rent a car, only to find that his credit card is over the limit. Eight years later this man, Barack Obama, is the elected the 44th president of the United States.

That vignette encapsulates the remarkable journey that this man, "son of a father from Kenya and a mother from Kansas," has taken from humble roots to extraordinary heights. Along the way, he has discovered how to balance his heritage in ways that that enabled him to build bridges to both cultures and in the process find himself at a nexus in history, the first African American president. It also demonstrates the sense of confidence, not to mention resilience, he has demonstrated his entire life.

An accomplished student, Obama graduated from Columbia University and later attended Harvard Law School, where he became the school's very first African American editor of the law review. That position demonstrated his ability to gravitate toward the center. He befriended the conservatives on the journal while sometimes annoying his more liberal colleagues, the ones who had helped him get elected. Upon graduation from law school, he passed up an opportunity to earn big money with a major law firm. Instead he returned to the streets of Chicago where he had been a community organizer. He practiced law and wooed his wife, Michelle, also a Harvard Law graduate, who did work for a major firm and later succeeded in becoming a successful corporate executive.

Politics beckoned, and he found himself running and winning a seat in the Chicago legislature. He later made a run for Congress in 2000 against Bobby Rush, a former Black Panther and now a Chicago political power. He lost, and fortunately for him he did. Two years later, he made a run for the U.S. Senate and won. During the senatorial campaign, Obama made a national name for himself at the 2004 Democratic convention where he gave a rousing speech about our nation not being "red states or blue states, but the United States."

His Senate career was more memorable for what he did not do: become an effective senator. However, Obama did use the Senate as a strategic launching site for his political future. He selected as his chief of staff Peter Rouse, former chief of staff for Senate Majority Leader, Tom Daschle. From Rouse, Obama learned how Washington worked and made connections with his party's political establishment. And when opportunity beckoned in the form of a presidential run, Obama grabbed it. His campaign began on the steps of the courthouse in Springfield, Illinois, the same place Abraham Lincoln had launched his campaign for the presidency of 1860.

Obama's extraordinary campaign took him to nearly every state. Along the way, he overcame a lack of resources and in the process built what some have called the best-run campaign of modern political history. What is remarkable about the campaign was Obama's active engagement. He had trusted aides to manage, but he made the critical decisions, and he set the tone for the campaign by being open and frank with the media as well as insisting that things within the campaign be kept running smoothly and efficiently. "No drama Obama" was the watchword. His campaign raised an unprecedented amount of money, over $750 million, more than any other campaign. Much of the funds came from small donors, but big-name donors were enlisted, too. In the process he overcame the Clinton machine, one with initially all the big endorsements and big donors. By going to the grassroots and campaigning online, Obama's anti-war message caught fire, and he ended up beating Senator Hillary Clinton in a closely fought race.

The campaign against John McCain seems in retrospect a slam dunk. After all, McCain was the standard bearer for the Republican Party that voters had deemed responsible not only for the unpopular war but also the faltering economy. Capping it off, President George W. Bush was one of the most unpopular presidents in history. Yet not until the economy tanked in September 2008 did it seem that Obama would win. Running as he did on a strong economy policy, backed by an ability to stick to his positions, he persevered.

Obama's heritage may make him liberal, but due in part to his biracial heritage and his collaborative spirit, he is less an idealist than a "political pragmatist." While he can deliver speeches that draw huge crowds and dazzle us with inspirational refrains, he is much more a roll-up-the-shirt-sleeves doer. Rhetoric is a means to an end, not an end to itself.

The challenges facing Obama as he took office in January 2009 were overwhelming. His first hundred days, as well as the seventy-five days he served as president-elect, demonstrated that he is a person who knows himself and his capabilities. He has surrounded himself with not merely a "team of rivals," but a team of individuals who are strong-willed and capable, the kind of people not afraid to present contrarian views. At the same time, Obama is the kind of leader who is secure enough in himself so that he can execute his vision. He admitted on election night 2008 that he would make mistakes but that he would do his best to lead the entire nation, not those who had voted for him, but the entire nation. History will be his judge.[2]

What Barack Obama Teaches Us About Leading Up:

- Believe in yourself first before you can lead others.
- Do not let adversity hold you back; use it to make you stronger.
- Put yourself forward as the go-to leader and watch what can happen.

■ ■ ■

Resilience is the capacity to withstand a setback and recover enough to stay in the game. Barack Obama could have thrown in the towel any number of times in his life. Resilience is about getting knocked down and getting up again. One of the reasons we introduce our children to youth sports is to teach them resilience. We want them to compete against their peers in ways that will enable them to discover their own strengths, both mental and physical. They will experience the exhilaration of victory as well as the pain of loss. Leading from the middle requires a great deal of resilience, because those in middle are so often thwarted in their efforts to effect positive change. Therefore, resilience is essential to sustaining their ability to lead. In a previous chapter (Step 1) we addressed the need for energy to drive enthusiasm. Resilience is a form of energy that lends the individual the gumption to fight for his ideas as well as to bounce back from defeat.

For example, coaches are forever looking for players with toughness. What they really mean is resilience. Lloyd Carr, former head football coach at the University of Michigan, recalls seeing a young Tom Brady compete in spring practice in full-speed drills.

Brady was repeatedly knocked down but always got up. Carr did not know the full extent of his quarterback's talents, but he knew that Brady was a gamer.[3] Tom Brady showed resilience then and throughout his professional career; in seven years he led the New England Patriots to three Super Bowl titles. It is often how players respond to those difficulties where they will learn their greatest lessons, that is, how to cope, recover, and regroup to compete again. These same lessons apply to the management arena.

Be Resilient

Resilience is essential to leadership from the middle. So often leadership is needed not when things are going well, but then things are going, or have gone, bad. It is times like this that you need a leader to rise up, look the odds in the eye, and persevere. While it is true that resilience is likely innate, it is important that leaders communicate it. Their communication does two things: One, it demonstrates strength in the face of adversity; two, it raises confidence in followers that they will fight for their beliefs. Here are some ways to encourage resilience in the workplace.

KNOW THE ODDS

It takes a leader with a good sense of self to survey the landscape and assess the chances for success as well as for failure. The concept of SWOT analysis (Strengths, Weaknesses, Opportunities, Threats) demands this discipline. Leaders who look at the odds, even though formidable, owe it to their people to communicate them. One of the terrible legacies of World War I was that generals were perpetually sending their troops in frontal assaults without hope of success. Such generals knew the odds but refused to face them. By contrast, aeronautical designer Burt Rutan, who has designed scores of aircraft, including one that flew nonstop around the world, acknowledges the odds but uses his aviation expertise and experience to surmount them. Such knowledge and daring led him to develop the first successful privately funded suborbital flight into space in 2004.

Acknowledge Failure

The truism that failure is a great teacher is all too often cast by the wayside. Sometimes the only way to succeed is to fail first. We seem to accept this fact in physical activities. Home repair do-it-yourselfers may be adept at plumbing a bathroom or rewiring a closet light switch, but they were not born doing it; they learned from others, and often through trial and error. Somehow in management we forget the learning curve and expect perfection immediately. This leads to projects that prematurely stall or to teams being disbanded before they have the opportunity to click. CEO of Starbucks, Howard Schultz, keeps copies of a publication, *Joe*, that the company bankrolled; it was an utter failure. The copies serve as reminders of failure but also of the need to keep going.[4] Acknowledging the odds and the setbacks can lead to learning lessons.

Turn Setbacks into Comebacks

Jeff Garcia, an NFL journeyman quarterback who has overcome injuries as well as criticism, says that he draws his motivation from people who believe he is not good enough to succeed. Graduating from San Diego State, he migrated to the Canadian Football League; success there got him the attention of NFL scouts, where he landed a starting quarterback job with the 49ers and later a succession of other NFL teams, including the Philadelphia Eagles and Tampa Bay Buccaneers. He has gotten teams into the playoffs and earned himself Pro Bowl honors.[5]

It is not only athletes who find motivation from nay-sayers. Belief in yourself is paramount to success. If you have talent and skills, and are willing to work hard, you can achieve dreams, despite the critics. You want to listen to constructive criticism and learn from it, but you must shut out the babble, criticism that is unfounded and ungrounded. Draw strength from what you do well and you can succeed.

SOLICIT IDEAS FOR COMEBACKS

Few leaders have all the answers, and sometimes not any answers. What good leaders possess is the willingness to ask questions and seek solutions. You might hear a suggestion here and another there and by piecing them together you come up with the makings of a solution that could make the project succeed. But this can only occur if you communicate, that is, listen and learn as leaders must do. For example, the idea for frappuccino, a cold coffee concoction, came from a Starbuck's store manager. CEO Howard Schultz paid attention, and it now generates hundreds of millions of dollars in revenue in both in-store and packaged versions sold in supermarkets.[6]

READ STORIES OF ADVERSITY

Just as failure can be a good teacher for yourself, its lessons can be taught to others. So too can stories about how individuals and teams overcame the odds, persevered, and won. Russell Simmons, the entertainment and fashion entrepreneur, talks about trying to get his hip-hop music label started. Record companies, both black and white, turned him down. He persisted, and in the process built an empire that prides itself on being an authentic voice of urban youth.[7] Startup companies need to share such stories because while their venture might be new, chances are that it is comprised of many veterans with good stories to share. Sharing such stories inspires confidence and illustrates what can be accomplished when people refuse to accept no right away.

As a young man, according his biographer Geoffrey C. Ward, Franklin Roosevelt was driven by a need to succeed. Our picture of him today is as our supremely confident leader, but his was not always that way. Franklin's role model was his cousin, Theodore

Roosevelt. Franklin admitted to his friends that he wanted to become president someday. And while he was popular, he did not impress anyone his age, nor in particular those who hired him as a young lawyer, as more than an affable young man. To use a contemporary term, he would have been perceived as a "lightweight." As a young man in the New York State Senate, he had the tenacity and courage to take on party bosses who held a stranglehold on his party, but he was not overly successful and gained few political allies as a result. Rather, it was Roosevelt's life-threatening bout with polio that altered his life; the disease forced him to rely upon his inner character. While such a disability would have forced others to withdraw from public life, it had precisely the opposite effect on Roosevelt. The experience liberated him and allowed him to fulfill his dreams. He became the fully self-confident president who leveraged that inner strength and sunny optimism to guide our nation through some of its most perilous years.[8]

Keep Your Cool

It is often said that crisis is what separates the pretenders from the leaders. A leader who maintains equilibrium during moments of high stress is one who will engender the respect of those she works with. This is especially true of one leading from the middle who is being observed by those in positions above and below her. Behavior in extremis reveals character. For example, if a firefighter loses all sense of reality when he enters a burning building — a natural reaction for all of us non-firefighters — then he probably should not be put in a position of dousing flames, nor should he be leading others into the inferno. That said, a first timer might want to run away — again a natural reaction — but if he is led by a strong and capable leader, he will find ways to maintain a cool head under trying circumstances. Likewise, if a young manager implodes at the first roadblock she encounters, she is not exhibiting behavior that will build trust. Her reaction may alternately frighten her associates and in time likely bore them. Most damaging is that they will not trust her.

Maintaining composure is essential to leadership presence. Some people, such George Washington or Winston Churchill, take to danger readily; both young men experienced hostile fire at an early age and both wrote something to effect of feeling calm when bullets intended for them missed. Others of us are not so fortunate. "None but a coward," said Marshal Ferdinand Foch, "dares to boast that he has never known fear." Learning to cope with fear comes from training, and it is essential for anyone commanding in extreme situations, be it the battlefield or the city streets. Likewise, training on the job for managers is essential to teach them how to handle adversity. None of us knows how we will handle tough situations until we face them. Training simply provides a foundation upon which to frame a reaction, e.g., if a sniper appears, take cover. Of if a product fails at launch, talk to your customers first. What actually happens depends upon circumstance and experience. During the actual moment of crisis, however, people will look to their leaders for guidance. And in that instance you must maintain equilibrium. If you do not, people will lose faith, or ultimately panic. And then the situation becomes more dire. There are some specifics to maintain.

Remain Calm

Who hasn't heard this one? But how do you remain cool when everything around you is going to hell? You distance yourself from the situation temporarily; you draw perspective on the moment. Tell yourself that this could have happened, but rather than dwell on the chaos, consider the next steps. Focusing energy into what you do takes you away from the panic of the moment. For example, if you have just learned that a deadline has been cut in half and your team has to work double-time to meet it, the easy thing to do would be to rail against your boss, the customer, or the "system."

But what good would that do? You focus on what you must do next. Get your people together and plan for the next steps.

Keep Your Voice Steady

Your voice is the dead giveaway for emotion. When things are easy, your voice is easy going and smooth. But when crises strike, the natural reaction is one of the following: one, stark barking commands; two, speaking in clipped sentences that allow for no rebuttal; or three, shifting into shrillness, where every word you utter sounds like you're hurtling down a rollercoaster. Leaders cannot afford to indulge in such voice hysterics. Keep your voice low and speak in measured tones. Even though your heart may be racing, speak calmly. Those who work with horse trainers know how to get an animal's attention; speak softly and the animal will respond. Shout and the animal will panic. Keep your voice down, and people will respond to the warmth. They are seeking reassurance and will be looking to you to give it.

Listen to People Frequently

Crises happen quickly, but they can also happen over time. In either situation, people want to see their leader; they want him or her near. Therefore, the leader who is present is an asset. You can triple your value if you take the time to listen to people. Sometimes you listen to learn about the situation; front-line people often know what is happening better than anyone else. Other times, especially during times of prolonged extremis, be it a night or a month, you listen to a person's heart, that is, you let him tell you what he's thinking about and why. It is a moment of intimacy that does a great deal to calm the situation as well as build greater levels of trust.

Of course, leaders are entitled, and even expected at times, to demonstrate urgency during crisis. If the building is on fire, the commander on the scene cannot tolerate laggards. She may have to raise her voice upon occasion to get someone's attention. During hurricane Katrina, the beleaguered mayor, Ray Nagin, vented at the federal government's lack of response to his city. He lost his cool, and it was captured on the airwaves. That is understandable, and frankly his reaction garnered national attention. It brought the plight of his city to the forefront, and soon after, troops were sent into restore order and bring urgently needed supplies.

But most often leaders need to keep their emotions in check. Flying off the handle frightens people and siphons away the sense of authority a leader needs to exert in times of crisis. Keeping it under control, however, does not mean the leader is impervious to the situation. No, it means he is sublimating his natural reaction for the good of others. Leaders in extremis realize that if they lose it, they may lose not only the respect and trust, but also further authority to lead. For leaders in battle situation, that loss of authority could be fatal. For leaders in business, that erosion of authority could compound already compromised situations with customers. Furthermore, when leaders lose it, they also damage their credibility, and once that is lost, it takes a near heroic effort to restore it.[9]

Manage the No

"Do not permit what you cannot do to get in the way of what you can do," says John Wooden, the legendary basketball coach whose UCLA basketball teams won ten NCAA titles in twelve years, a feat that is unlikely to be matched again.[10] The advice is not only applicable to athletes but especially to middle managers. Jim Collins, the management guru and author of the monograph "Good to Great and the Social Sector," recalls a senior leader at a university saying that managing in such a decentralized structure was "leading a thousand points of no!" While power is more centralized in a corporate structure, there are always more people who can say no than people who can say yes. The secret to managing in such an environment is to understand what you can do, and do it, as well as what you cannot do, and move on.[11] Middle managers must deal with peers or superiors who say no to their faces with regularity. So what's a leader who must get something done to do? Here are some suggestions.

REGARD THE FIRST NO AS AN INVITATION

There is, however, virtue in not taking no for the first answer. Part of the process of developing an idea or a project is to counter objections. When people say no the first time, consider it an invitation for discussion. Ask the nay-sayer for time to explain your case; be courteous about it, even a little deferential as in, "I know you have a busy schedule, but could you spare a half-hour? There are some points I want to make certain that I have made clear." This opens doors to less debate and more dialogue.

FRAME YOUR ARGUMENT IN TERMS OF ORGANIZATIONAL NEED

Every decision about people and resources within an organization should be determined on the basis of need and value. Nice to say, but how often this mantra is followed is highly debatable given the number of clock-watching employees or value-detracting make-do projects there are in every organization. But when you are making your case, focus not on personal need but on what the team needs. For example, use the business case to demonstrate the benefits that this project will deliver to customers and in turn to the organization. A mention of how this project will make senior executives look good is always a plus. One way to ensure this bit of sunshine is to get the top people on your side, get them to support your project.

GO AROUND THE NO CLEVERLY

People who work for micro-managers live in a world of constant no. Their bosses are forever meddling in their business. Not only is this behavior annoying, it is wholly unproductive. The micro-manager is not managing, only meddling. The challenge for employees is to provide the meddler with something to sink his teeth into so he can while away the hours. Experienced employees will dump detailed analyses on the boss's desk to keep him occupied. Then, while the boss has his fingers tangled in columns of numbers, they will go off and do what needs doing. The truth is that the micro-manager should never be allowed to manage, but he is, so savvy employees find ways around his nos.

Go Along with the No

Organizations are made stronger by people lobbying for what they believe in. We need managers with backbone to stand up for what they believe, otherwise they are simply ticket punchers, or yes people who prefer to roll with the tide. Some managers simply say no the first time to every proposal that comes their way, not because they are negative or contrary, but because they want to test the mettle of the person proposing the idea. They, like General Eisenhower, understand that "it's not the size of the dog that matters, but rather the size of fight in the dog." If you want it, fight for it, and in the process show us what you and your idea or project can do for the organization.

Few of us will get many points for giving up. "Defeating those negative instincts that are out to defeat us is the difference between winning and losing," said Olympic athlete and civil rights pioneer, Jesse Owens. "And we face that battle every day of our lives." Perseverance and persistence for the right issue and the right cause is a matter of leadership.

Know When to Say No

Resilience is not without limits. When you are leading up and are faced with overwhelming odds, you need to know when to back down and wait for another opportunity. Otherwise, every argument will lead to a kind of Armageddon, reminiscent of the battle scenes that occur in the climax of the third film in the *Lord of the Rings* trilogy — plenty of mayhem and destruction. Resilience must be tempered with patience and forbearance. Patience to know that your time and your ideas for implementation may come again. And forbearance to withhold the metaphorical torch that you are aching to use on the last remaining "bridge" that spans the gap between you and your boss.

Mark Cuban parlayed a sale of his Internet company, Broadcast.com, into a multibillion-dollar fortune. A self-made entrepreneur, Cuban was fired from several jobs and found himself sharing an apartment with six other guys. Cuban slept on the floor. Today he is the flamboyant but hands-on owner of the NBA's Dallas Mavericks as well as an investor in a number of other businesses. For Cuban, ideas are only a starting point; "Sweat equity is the most important capital." That means you invest yourself in the business and make it work.[12]

Treat People with Fairness and Equality

There is another side of resilience that pertains to middle management: the need to be tough for the good of your organization. Our Constitution, the legal framework upon which our nation was established, ensures equality in terms of gender, ethnicity, conditions, and treatment. It does not, however, mandate that bosses treat performance equally. Good performance must be demonstrated and managers ensure that it is maintained.

Let me illustrate with a story goes something like this: Say you are the owner of a restaurant, and the hostess comes in late; you fire her. If a waitress is tardy, you dock her an hour's pay. If the cook is tardy, you raise your voice in reprimand. Here's the kicker. If the dishwasher strolls in an hour past clock-in time, you get him a cup of coffee, sit him down at the table, and ask, "What's going on? Anything I can do for you?" Why would an owner do this? Because you don't want to spend the night washing dishes! That story was laughingly told to me by Paul Saginaw, co-owner of the Zingerman's, a community of food businesses that *Inc.* magazine once dubbed, "America's coolest small company." Saginaw uses the story to illustrate exactly what he does differently. He and partner, Ari Weinzweig, treat their employees equitably, but not always equally. Zingerman's is a business built on principles of treating workers honestly, compassionately, and fairly. Performance is rewarded, and opportunities open up for people who perform well.[13]

Fairness must be a cornerstone value of every enterprise; so too is equality. Every employee deserves the right to be provided the tools, resources, and conditions to succeed. However, when employees outperform the standards, they deserve recognition and reward, be it in the form of a bonus, a raise, or a promotion. Yet discussions with managers show time after time that managers often end up mistreating top performers while rewarding underperformers, like the tardy dishwasher. Why? Sometimes, as in the case of the dishwasher, an underperformer is doing a job no one else wants to do. Or more often it's because the manager feels sorry for the laggard and in a misguided way lets the slacker off the hook. This same manager, by contrast, may ignore the top achievers. Why? Because he doesn't want them getting swelled heads. Sad, but true. So what can you do to treat employees fairly and performance differently?

CLARIFY YOUR TERMS

Distinguish between fairness and equality as it relates to people and performance. You provide fair and equal opportunities for everyone; furthermore, you must regard all performances fairly. That is, performance appraisals are not conditional upon personality, — whether you like someone. You judge performance within the context of the job and reward accordingly. Most employees understand the distinction but it is always good to remind them from time to time.

Integrate Fairness into Change

Life ain't always fair, that's a fact certainly. But managers owe it to their employees to be fair in all dealings, particularly when it comes to performance evaluations. Often, performance objectives are set early in the year. Those objectives may be challenging, but they should be attainable. What happens, however, is that changing conditions internally or externally necessitate change, so employees are given new priorities or even new reporting assignments. What fails to keep up is the performance objective process; new objectives never seem to become written objectives. So when the employee is evaluated, in particular by a boss who came on board during the year, she may not meet the stated objectives because her responsibilities changed. Strange as it may seem, the employee is held more accountable for what she did not do than what she did do, even when she was ordered to do something else. Therefore, managers owe it to their employees to keep real-time track of objectives and metrics so that performance is evaluated fairly.

Promote the Stars

Just as underperformers may be asked to show improvement, those who achieve should have opportunities for advancement, in pay, rank, or both. Treat those who produce well and the rest of the business will take care of itself. This is wholly fair. What is not fair is withholding opportunities for people to show their mettle. Fairness dictates that people be given resources and timelines to succeed. By extension, you want to give people who are performing opportunities to strive for a stretch objective. If they decline, fine, but you want to invite them to try. [You might also do the same for underperformers; sometimes the challenge serves as a wakeup call.] But when managers allow personality or personal likes and dislikes to get in the way, then that's unfair. Managers who promote "pets" over performers are not being fair or equitable.

Managers have an obligation to expect performance from employees. When an employee has what she needs to do the job right, and does, she has a right to expect equitable treatment, and perhaps even opportunity for advancement or increased compensation. Is this fair? Yes, she's earned it. Conversely, when an employee underperforms — and has all the necessities to do the job — he has no right to expect to be rewarded or promoted. That's fair, too. But if that person is in the wrong slot — say a salesperson who avoids people, or an accountant who can't compute — it is the manager's fault for putting him or her there in the first place. That's neither fair nor equitable. So who's accountable? The manager, of course! And when consequences result from an employee's inability to perform, the dime drops on the manager. Leading from the middle requires the ability to balance fairness and equality as well as the will to act on principle for the good of the organization.

Remember That Resilience Matters

Doing good for the organization requires resilience because you are pushed and pulled by forces above and below you. Remember then that resilience is rooted in your character; it dictates how you think and act. Every successful leader, especially those in the middle, has dealt with adversity. The bigger the challenges surmounted, the greater the reservoirs of resilience. The challenges to our resilience are constant throughout every phase of our lives. How we rebound and cope with them marks our character as well as our capacity to lead. Recall the Latin proverb by Perseus, "He conquers who endures." The courage to continue — your inner motivation — propels you forward and makes you a leader that others want to follow now and in the future.

What You Need to Do to Bend but Not Break

You need to demonstrate resilience. Life comes at you from different directions. Sometimes it comes so hard it will knock you down. There is no shame in falling; what matters is getting up to fight again. And when your people see you doing that, they will be encouraged to follow your example. This example can be used to demonstrate an ability to lead the entire organization, not simply the boss.

To bend but not break, you will need to:

- Know the odds. Avoid tackling projects where the odds of success are overwhelmingly against you.
- Acknowledge failure but do not dwell on it.
- Do your own after-action review. Examine what went right as well as what went wrong.
- Turn setbacks into comebacks. Learn what you did wrong and how you can turn it around the next time.
- Exert strength (and exude it, too). Let others see how you are holding fast to your principles even though you may have failed to accomplish an immediate goal.

PREPARING OTHERS TO LEAD

The people at the so-called bottom of an organization
know more about what's going on than the people at the
top. . . . It's up to leaders to give those people the
freedom and the resources that they need.
MARTIN SORRELL, CEO, WPP GROUP[1]

Tim Russert, moderator of NBC's *Meet the Press*, was one of the
toughest journalists on the air. While his reputation for fair-
minded journalism is well known, what is less well known is his
legacy as a leader. Not only was he an on-air host, he was the
Washington bureau chief of NBC News. As such, he served as a
planner of news coverage as well as manager of some of the bureau's brightest stars, including David Gregory, Chuck Todd, and
Andrea Mitchell.

As judged by extensive coverage of Russert's untimely death of
a heart attack at 58, Russert was deeply admired, better yet, treasured by his colleagues. Russert had joined the bureau as an executive and later became an on-air talent. Mitchell referred to him a
"player-manager" who was able to help colleagues from a vantage
of reporting stories along with those he supervised. And so it is fit-
ting to remember something of Russert's management style.

Russert loved politics. As an attorney and former political operative, Russert knew how politicians thought and acted. As a former aide to Senator Daniel Patrick Moynihan and Governor Mario Cuomo, Russert understood and respected politicians. A registered independent, Russert was tough on politicians on both sides of the aisle. Being on *Meet the Press* was de rigueur for any pol on the way up, or any pol who wanted to remain there.

His friend, Bob Schieffer, moderator of rival CBS's *Face the Nation*, said that Russert was like a "quarterback who could see the whole field" as it pertained to politics. He saw the big picture and therefore was able to direct coverage of it and to provide proper analysis. He also shared that knowledge with his colleagues. Colleague Chris Matthews said that Russert was always willing to share what he knew; getting it right was more important than beating the other guy.

Russert applied the vigorous research ethic of a prosecuting attorney. He wanted to know both sides of the issue and ask the questions that viewers might wonder, or better yet, ask those that no one might think of in order to bring an issue to light or a politician into sharper view. His fairness in journalism extended to his colleagues. He expected them to hold to the highest standards. He also supported them. At the foot of his desk is a sign that includes the admonition "no whining." Russert made it clear that working in television journalism was a privilege, and he held his fellow reporters to the same high standards he held himself.

Tom Brokaw, former NBC anchor, recalled that he would occasionally send Russert young men and women who were interested in politics and journalism. Russert would inevitably find an internship for them, and then provide guidance post-internship to see that they were headed in the right direction. That personal investment in others extended to so many of his colleagues. Russert was forever phoning or sending messages to co-workers who had a new baby, an illness in the family, or were going through a tough time personally.

Russert is often remembered for his best-selling book, *Big Russ and Me*, the story of his upbringing and his deep relationship with his father, a garbage man who worked another full-time job to support his family and send the kids to Catholic school. A genuine family man, Russert also made his colleagues part of that family in a way that enhanced his profession as well as made life better for those around him.

Russert's style was summed up by his eventual successor at *Meet the Press*, moderator David Gregory, who was advised by Russert to "be respectful but ask the tough questions and think of the smart follow-up and hold them accountable. And if you come out that way and if you're fair, you'll be just fine in the end."[2]

What Tim Russert Teaches Us About Leading Up:
- Believe in your abilities to effect positive change.
- Develop the skills of others so they can achieve their potential.
- Live life to the fullest at work, at play, and at home.

■ ■ ■

To her life was a stage and the stage. After all, she first performed on radio at the tender age of 4, and years later on the stages of the grandest opera houses in the world. When she ceased her singing career, she took up another daunting role in management, first as general director of the New York City Opera and later as chairwoman for Lincoln Center. She was Beverly Sills, aka Bubbles.

Her nickname, given to her in childhood, says it all, and as her obituaries and remembrances from friends and colleagues note, she was "effervescent." She loved what she did and pursued it with great passion. A Brooklyn native, Miss Sills did not have things handed to her. She worked and scraped her way to the top of the opera world, first with New York City Opera and finally, after many decades of trying, she made it to the Metropolitan Opera. What a climb!

Leading an opera company is no lark. Operatic stars are not called prima donnas for nothing, and that includes the men, too. Likewise, opera fans are ruthless; they expect nothing short of perfection from their singers each and every time. High expectations are door openers. Opera fans expect the world. And so this puts managers — those who must contract the stars as well as lure the fans — often between a rock and hard place. Miss Sills handled the job with a mixture of business and artistic savvy, and a touch of populist diva. Sills was always a star. So what can we learn from her example?

Beverly Sills worked hard. While her career began on the commercial side (radio), she learned her operatic craft the traditional way — voice lessons, music school, and touring companies. It was a long slog; it was not until 1955 that she made it to City Opera. As she told *Newsweek*, "I had my first high heels, my first updo hair style, my first strapless dress, and I didn't know what to hold up first." And it took her another twenty years to sing at the Metropolitan Opera, after performing at London's Covent Garden and Milan's La Scala. Sometimes it's hard to be a star in your own hometown.

Sills did not doubt her talents. Reviews throughout her early career and into her mid-career were mixed and may have accounted for her not being called to the Met sooner. Still she sang. And it was that confidence that gave her the gumption (or guts) to say yes to running the debt-laden City Opera when she retired as a singer in 1980. She was born to the role. She used her charm and stage presence to lure the big donors and her public persona to lure the patrons. Show business was in her blood, and she knew how to merchandise with the best of them. She also had a wonderful sense of humor. When commenting on her successful debut at La Scala, Sills remarked, "It's probably because Italians like big women, big bosoms, and big backsides." Her ability to laugh with herself is a gift anyone struggling to succeed can appreciate.

Above all, Sills knew how to leverage stardom. Listening to her sing is to listen to a voice that clearly loves music. And she had the ability to invite others to share it with her, serving as a bridge between the world of opera and popular entertainment. She appeared many times on the *Tonight Show* with Johnny Carson and even won an Emmy with friend Carol Burnett for a program that blended comedy and music. She also hosted PBS's *Live from Lincoln Center.*

Sills also used her star power for "her twin causes of medical research and music," recalled friend, Manuela Hoelteroff, executive editor of *Bloomberg's Muse.* Hoelteroff reckons Sills raised at least $80 million for the March of Dimes and notes she left the once financially stripped City Opera with an endowment of $5 million. While it has been decades since Sills sang in public, the purity and beauty of her lovely voice is very evident on her many recordings. Listening to them, you will catch a glimpse of a woman who knows her craft and loves it all the more.[3]

What Beverly Sills Teaches Us About Leading Up:

- Use your talent as a stepping stone to achieve.
- Know your strengths because they can help you overcome difficulties.
- Learn to achieve good things by leveraging the talents of others.

■ ■ ■

Coach Paul "Bear" Bryant (whom we met in Step 3) had three rules about winning. Among the most successful coaches of all time, Bryant focused first on getting the right players and coaches and then on being prepared mentally and physically, e.g., "have a plan for everything." The glue between these rules was his second principle: "Be able to recognize winners. They come in all forms."[4] This is something that Tim Russert and Beverly Sills understood well. As creative people (reporter/author and singer, respectively) both individuals, like Bear Bryant, had an uncanny eye for spotting talent.

Like all successful coaches, Bryant was generous with praise as well as gracious in defeat. This rule, however, goes deeper than lauding talent; it includes identifying and nurturing it. Every player who played for Bryant was not a superstar. Bryant prided himself on getting players to work hard and play above themselves. In his autobiography, he wrote, "If my 75% (player) plays 15% over his ability and your 100% (player) slogs around and plays 15% under his, then we'll beat you every time." Bryant's second rule of recognition has implications far off the gridiron; it is one reason why we still remember him two decades after he coached his last game.[5] This rule is something that those who desire to lead up must not only realize but actualize. While much of this book has focused on what it takes to prepare self to lead up, part of that self must give way to leading others. That is why it is so critical for leaders on the way up to recognize and surround themselves with talented individuals.

Leading up requires the ability to develop the talents of others; this is important for two reasons. One, you need to demonstrate that you know how to lead others; and two, putting others into leadership positions gives you the time you need to think and act strategically, that is, to lead your boss and your team more effectively. Senior leaders value these skills, thus it is critical that you practice them so that you prove you are ready and prepared to assume roles of greater significance and importance as your career progress.

Differentiate Between Talent and Skill

Developing others begins with learning how to differentiate between talent and skills. In this I defer to the definition that Marcus Buckingham and Curt Coffman use in their book, *First Break All the Rules*. According to these two consultants from the Gallup Organization, talent is the proclivity for doing something; skill is your ability to do it. The two are not synonymous. For example, an engineer has a talent for uncovering why things are the way they are. His skill set is the processes he has mastered to analyze and problem solve. Putting him in a situation where he can apply his skill set to diagnose problems and devise solutions is ideal. On the other hand, if you put this engineer in a sales role where he must call on customers all day, the situation is less than ideal. Finding the right slot for this engineer is the job of management. Often the biggest challenges in management are dealing with people who have been placed in the wrong slots.[6]

Some managers have a say about whom they put on their team; other managers (perhaps the majority) are handed the full roster. Regardless, it is up to the manager to discover the talent and skills within and do what she can to develop them. Management today is a balance between taking care of business and taking care of people. Good managers realize that if you take care of people, the business takes care of itself. Therefore, you have to use the talent that you have to get things done, and done right. Here are some suggestions.

Look Under the Surface

We are all familiar with the way coaches move players from one position to another; for example, a running back becomes a defensive back, or a receiver becomes a safety. When those position swaps work, it is a credit to the coach who took the time to evaluate each player and match according to team need. The same rule applies to managers. Employees may hire in at one level but in time develop skills that are best suited elsewhere. They will never get the opportunity to move, however, if they are not asked.

Look into Their Souls

John W. Gardner, former statesman and author, said, "When hiring key employees, there are only two qualities to look for, judgment and taste. Almost everything else can be bought by the yard."[7] Such an individual radiates energy and enthusiasm and is hungry to contribute as well as to learn. Such people are ones you want on your team; they add the spark that kicks projects into gear. They are also the people you want to groom for future leadership positions. Their vigor, coupled with capacity for discovery, makes them ideal people to lead; leadership demands energy as well as applied knowledge that comes from self and others.

Cross Train

One reason why companies push cross training is because it ensures redundancy in case one or more people are unable to work; managers can take comfort in knowing that other people can do the job. From a developmental standpoint, cross training is essential to professional growth. By learning different jobs, you keep yourself from growing stale, and you also you expand your skill set and often your own horizons. Doing another job is like visiting another part of the country; you see, hear, and learn new things. You may wish to return to your original job, but at least you have tried something different, a task that may have taught you valuable skills or taught you that you are best at your current job. That's a valuable lesson, too.

Create Challenges

All of us like our comfort zones; it is where we are productive. But in an organization where things change rapidly, your comfort zone is someone else's target of opportunity. Therefore, it is up to the manager to challenge her people by pushing them to develop their skills and tackle more demanding roles of responsibility. The manager does this by coaching them and discovering what they are capable of doing and what they want to do. Such challenges are not for everyone, but for those people looking to move up the ladder, such challenges are welcome opportunities.

Find the Right Slot

When someone on your team is not working out, do not discard them like used paper towel, find another place for them. Very often the best things managers have done for their employees is transfer them to a job where they can excel. The person with high social skills may be happy in sales, or the person in sales who likes doing reports may be happy in accounting. That's matching talent for talent.

Finding talent is something every manager in the middle must do, but if you cannot recruit it, you must learn to live with what you have. When this happens, the management equilibrium tilts more heavily to the people side. Managers become like magicians trying to pull rabbits out of their hats. But it is not magic; it is hard work trying to make things work when you do not have the right people to do the job. This situation can work for a short term, but with time, the system breaks down, most often because the manager has run out of hats or rabbits, or both.

Recognition of talent, of course, includes giving people credit for a job well done. That is what we mean most often by "recognition," but it is good also to recall Coach Bryant's wording of his rule: "Be able to recognize." That phrase makes you the chief talent scout, one looking for people who can work hard and win if they are put in a position to do.

Harness the Talent

Identifying talent is one thing; you have to put that talent to work. One hot summer evening I accompanied my then 16-year-old daughter and her friend to a local ice cream franchise outlet. The place was packed to the walls with a mixture of parents with young children as well as young adults and teens. Normally, I would have turned tail and sought another place, but my daughter liked the product, so we stayed. I am glad I did, because behind the counter I saw an example of teamwork in action. There were eight people working behind the counter; each one was taking orders and filling them. What could have been chaos was a choreography of good service, good product, and, yes, good cheer. But here's the kicker: Everyone behind the counter looked to be a teenager. Later, in a conversation, with the manager, I learned that a couple of the workers were age 20; the rest were teens. In a day and age when teens are mostly dumped on for being lazy and useless, this team's work ethic was notable. They were a salient example of a self-led team; they pushed and pulled together as one efficient unit, and they made it fun for the customers.

A salient feature of a high-performance team is its ability to lead itself. While many organizations pride themselves on pushing for leadership at all levels, one aspect that is often overlooked is the responsibility for teams and individuals to lead themselves. As with horses to water, you can appoint people to lead, but you cannot make them pick up the reins. You have to want to lead. Team leadership is based upon peer example. When one member of the team sees another doing the heavy lifting, he or she may be inclined to pitch in. Or, conversely, if one or two members slack off, it gives license for others to do the same. Team cohesion is rooted in the concept of all for one and one for all. Here are suggestions to develop it.

EMPHASIZE TEAM

Every organization preaches teamwork. However, saying it is one thing, practicing it is another. Managers who want to nurture teamwork need to communicate the need for it. How? If the team concept already exists, talk up results at staff meetings. Discuss what the teams have achieved and what they plan to do next. If teams do not exist, consider building them. Talk is cheap, so managers need to stimulate teamwork by putting people in positions where they can collaborate. Ask people how they feel about working in teams. Teams may not be for everyone, but teamwork in the sense of collaboration is essential to any organization.

SHARE THE LEAD

If you want teams to demonstrate leadership, give them the power. It is not enough to confer responsibility; the team must have the authority to do the job. As part of the process, you may wish to let the team designate its own team leader, much as athletic teams vote for captains. This is not always possible, but it is a good example of delegating genuine responsibility. Let the team divvy up roles and responsibilities. Monitor the results. As part of the sharing process, debrief the team. Ask people what went right as well as what they would want to do better. Technology companies keep a record of these pluses and minuses as a means of improvement. Again, that is a form of responsibility and leadership.

REINFORCE THE LEAD

A shining example of teamwork is the Detroit Red Wings, winners of four Stanley Cups, the NHL's championship, in twelve years. That team concept stems in part from Ken Holland, a former minor league hockey player now general manager. It was reinforced by coach Mike Babcock, who has shepherded the team for three seasons. But, most important, it comes from the team itself. They police themselves; they create expectations and fulfill them. They are personal leaders who believe in working together as a team. They have discovered that team leadership is based upon personal leadership; they have leveraged individual responsibility to team commitment. As individuals, they were skilled players; as Wings, they are winners.

Provide Leadership for the Team

Developing leaders requires providing a strong example for them to follow. All organizations need the guidance of leaders who set the direction. Those leaders also are in place to make the tough decisions. The responsibility for ensuring consistency in quality and service falls to the manager, but it also falls to the team that reinforces the practices and behaviors that make the team click and its customers satisfied. To cultivate a leadership ethos you must demonstrate it yourself. Consider:

SET THE RIGHT EXAMPLE

If you want people to lead, show them how. Be an example by demonstrating leadership in big things. For example, communicate intentions clearly and often. Set standards and ensure that everyone knows them. Do not forget to do the small things. Again, recognize achievement in a timely manner. Let people know how you feel about them and keep doing it.

REWARD MISTAKES OF GOOD INTENTION

All of us make mistakes. Turn the mistakes into leadership lessons. Call a meeting to find out what went wrong and why. Ask the persons responsible to explain why they did what they did. But make certain this is a collaborative process, not a call on the carpet. Ask them, and others, what they have learned and what they would do differently the next time.

MAKE IT KNOWN THAT LEADERSHIP MATTERS

When you see things out of whack, make a comment. If people fail to show up on time for work or meetings (and do not have a valid excuse), call them on it. Insist on timeliness and punctuality. Also, practice common courtesy toward others. Disagree over ideas, but not over personalities. When trouble does brew, address it immediately. The Salvation Army is a highly principled organization bound together by common purpose but guided by leaders who set the right example in all that they do.

Take a Leap of Faith

Developing another leader is an investment in the future. Once during an interview about leadership, a high-tech venture capitalist whose business it was to turn dreams into businesses told me that the toughest job in management was not the top job; it was becoming a first-line supervisor. This executive knew what he was talking about since he had once been a COO of a multibillion-dollar global computer company and was now advising small start-ups.[8]

Taking the first step into management requires a great leap of faith. Why? Because it means that you are leaving everything behind you have done to get yourself noticed. You move from the comfort zone where you are master of your domain, a technical wizard capable of making systems speak and networks sing, into an amorphous and murky area where dark shadows lurk and nothing may be as it seems — management. Why is this so? Those who succeed by virtue of technical virtuosity, be it writing coding or doing regression analyses, are educated in university and trained on the job to do their craft. They have the technical aptitude and practice it daily.

Few of us receive this kind of preparation for management. Even vaunted MBA programs spend more class time on the analytics (finance, accounting, strategy) than on the human dynamic. An article in *Strategy + Business*, based upon a study conducted by Booz Allen Hamilton, cited statistics showing that business schools were not preparing their people to lead, nor to communicate. Part of this deficiency is not the schools' fault; they are in business to teach the discipline of management. The dynamic that makes enterprises go are people. Teamwork in school, and throughout a business career, teaches people to learn to share and cooperate in order to get things done. That's where leadership and communications are learned. [Come to think of it, kindergarten teachers do much the same.][9]

Becoming a manager means you supervise. While much of management is administrative, it is by supervising that you move people and get results. Supervision is a balancing act between pushing and shoving as well as letting go. You are now responsible for the vision, planning, execution, and coaching of your people. The engine that drives these processes is communication. Here are some things to keep in mind as you supervise.

Make a Habit of Speaking Up

One excuse people make for managers who do not communicate is that they are shy people and don't like to speak up. That may be true, but if you choose to go into management, and yes it is a choice, you must speak up. This does not mean you have to emulate the oratory of a Ronald Reagan or Colin Powell, but it does mean you have to express your leadership point of view. By that we mean what you want your team to accomplish and why it is important to them and the organization. Be as explicit as possible and speak frequently.

Formalize Your Listening Process

Many supervisors think that as soon as they take the reins, they have to start making a slew of changes to put their stamp on the department. This may be necessary in the case of a failing business or a sinking department, but before you make any more changes than your name on the cubicle, take time to listen. Go around to people in the department and introduce yourself and ask them what they do. One athletic director at a major university did this and instantly won over the support of everyone. His predecessor had used his office as a bunker: firing out, but never inviting in.

Create a Learning Process

The outcome of speaking and listening needs to be learning. A manager of an engineering operation demonstrated his learning process through a series of breakfast meetings with everyone in the plant, from hourly to supervisory personnel. The first round of breakfast sessions were listening sessions; the second round were updates on what had been accomplished. By meeting in small groups, the manager was able to demonstrate that he had listened and had implemented some changes based upon what he had learned. Keep in mind, managers do not, nor should not, implement every suggestion made, but they need to consider and evaluate each one. By talking suggestions over with others and adding to them, good things can occur.

Humanize Supervision

Supervision is integral to management and is something that those leading up must practice daily. Supervision requires a deft touch as well as occasionally a swift kick. How you communicate can give you clues on when you nudge or when you back off. If an employee seems at sea on a problem, you have a conversation for three reasons: one, to find out what is going on work-wise and what actions you need to take to achieve results; two, to discover how your people think and act and what makes them tick; and three, to gain insight into yourself and what you need to do or not do the next time. This is what becoming a supervisor is all about. And you can only do it if you are willing to communicate.

Warren Bennis tells the story of his first leadership position. It occurred in the middle of the Ardennes Forest in the dead of winter in the midst of one of the fiercest engagements of World War II, the Battle of the Bulge. Bennis had just been appointed a second lieutenant, and he took command of a group of battle-hardened soldiers. He quickly realized that his future, not to mention that of his company, depended upon his learning from their experience and following the lead of his sergeant rather than imposing his own will. Gradually, he gained his men's trust, and they followed his lead. Bennis was all of 19.[10]

What happened to Bennis, who later became professor and president of the University of Cincinnati as well as a respected leadership author, occurs to many first-time managers, although the situation is seldom so dire. But the fear factor is there. For a newly promoted manager, there is always trepidation about the first time being in control. Those who have not been properly schooled in leadership or management will automatically assume that they must continue doing all they have been doing and tell everyone else what to do. It is honest assumption; managers are promoted on the basis of proficiency in their selected function, be it engineering, accounting, logistics, or marketing. And having never managed others, novice managers assume, perhaps because others over them have done so, that management is about *telling* people what to do. Managers also feel great pressure, stoked by fear of failure, that they must act quickly and impose their will swiftly and without opposition.

Management is about two things: one, controlling systems, and two, getting things done on time and on budget. Neither can occur without the heartfelt support of people on the team. Managers who try to do everything themselves end up working ungodly hours trying to juggle all the balls in the air; many burn out and quit in frustration. Management, therefore, requires a sharing of the load; in reality, it is about enabling others on the team to carry the load with the manager acting as coach and chief supporter.

The coaching analogy is a good one; just as coaches do not play the game; neither should managers do all of the work. They should provide the framework for others to do the work and then support them with resources and constant support. Communication is an operative driver in management, especially for first timers. Here are some suggestions.

Introduce and Engage

The biggest thing many managers omit to do is the easiest — introduce yourself. Some newcomers make the mistake of assuming that people know who they are and just proceed blithely unaware, occupying their offices as a newly acquired fiefdom. Such assumptions put people on edge. Successful managers make a habit of going around to everyone and introducing themselves. They also engage in conversation and get to know something about their people, e.g., family, work habits, and job preferences. First-time introductions may not be the ideal time to discuss ideas in depth, but this is a good time for the manager to make it known that she is open for input and ideas.

ADDRESS THE NEGATIVES

Few managers walk into a new department without challenges. The manager may be hired from the outside, may be younger than most on the team, or may have been promoted over others in the organization. None of these factors should have any bearing on the manager's competency, but unless they are addressed, and defused, they will fester and foster the development of factions, those for and against the new manager. Make it known right from the start that you want everyone's input and support and that you expect it. Furthermore, make it known that you will support them, too. For example, you can cozy up to a veteran by asking his advice in navigating bureaucracy. And when things go well, make certain he gets immediate credit.

INVITE EVERYONE INTO THE TENT

Factions, as mentioned, are an issue; seek to dispel them immediately. If you sense cliques developing, dissolve them. As a new manager, you have the luxury of "not knowing any better," so you can ask people who normally do not work together to do just that. Of course, if resistance is too great, then you may have to invite people to work solo, or perhaps leave your department. Management is a balancing act between bringing people together and finding and eliminating those who work against the team.

PROVE THAT YOU VALUE PEOPLE

Communicating that you value someone is one thing; proving it is another. So when people do a good job, let them know about it. Share the credit. Ask them what other assignments they might like. Engage them, as well as everyone, in discussions about work development. Managers owe it to their people to provide training as well as opportunities for professional growth. Former U.S. Navy Captain David Abrashoff writes in *It's Your Ship* that he made it possible for sailors on his ship to further their education by arranging for them to take the SAT on board the ship.

This act, coupled with legions of others, demonstrated Abrashoff's focus on his people. As a result, he improved re-enlistment rates significantly.[11]

Provide the Big Picture

Each of us has the tendency to focus more on the small picture (e.g., what we are doing) so that we lose sight of the big picture (what the entire organization is doing). You can become so wrapped up in details that you lose sight of what it is you are working for. Managers can correct this by providing context to department activities. One way to do this is by sharing stories of how your department's work is making things better for customers, internal and external. And when things are not going well, put them into context of what you need to do better. When you give people specific reasons for improvement, they begin to see their work as part of a larger whole and seek to do better. Saturn, once a division of General Motors, now owned by Penske Automotive Group, enabled factory workers and customers to meet and mingle; workers took pride in their handiwork when they saw how customers responded to what they had made.

Demonstrate Good Cheer

Yes, work is hard and sometimes tedious, but managers can do something about it. First, they must talk up the benefits of the work; for example, discuss how the team's efforts will enable the company to turn a profit and keep people employed. Second, managers can address ways to improve the work and find ways to do so. Third, managers can lighten up. Those in charge who crack jokes at their own expense or smile at people when they meet them project a positive attitude. Few of us can be upbeat all of the time, but if you make an attempt at lightness, people will respond positively. Such attitudes are not only healthy for the team, they are contagious; others will emulate your example.

Enable Others to Lead

The lesson for middle managers is this: When it comes to leadership, it's not about you; it's about us — the team! One of the failings in the corporate development process is the overemphasis on individual results. Once you are past the entrepreneurial phase, results come from the cooperation of others. Smartly managed organizations understand that the chief role of managers is to enable their teams; after all, it is the workers who produce results, not managerial solo acts. However, it is not manager's fault for thinking it is up to him or her. Performance reviews are based on what managers accomplish. Yet so often those results come from the collaboration of others pulling together to fulfill the vision, mission, and strategies.

Managers leading from the middle can leverage their communications to reach their people and demonstrate how important they are to the enterprise. Like a race driver to crew chief, chief to mechanic, and so on throughout the team, everyone pulls together to make the car run. The driver may push the pedals, but if there is nothing behind those pedals, that car looks good but goes nowhere. Here are some suggestions to improve the team concept.

Set the Course, Not the Agenda

People want to be pointed in the right direction, but they would like to navigate the direction by themselves. Managers can help by stating corporate vision and mission, then communicating how their department and its team contribute to that effort. When it comes to determining how to achieve it, employees will feel a greater sense of ownership if they can contribute the how. This how includes everything from writing performance objectives to setting metrics for objectives. Of course, the manager needs to buy into the process, but when employees take the lead, they demonstrate individual leadership, something that can only be good for the organization.

Encourage Alternatives

When managers take the lead, good ideas by employees are shunted aside. This may be appropriate in some situations, but when it comes to problem solving, you want all kinds of ideas floated, particularly when persistent problems occur. For example, those closest to the problem — be it engineers or customer service reps — know the causes as well as the cures. It is up to management to tap into their ideas. Some may not be feasible, but many suggestions may not only solve problems, but prevent them from occurring.

Step Aside So Others Can Take the Helm

The notion that managers should allow employees to run the department gets to the very essence of what it means to lead up. Such managers are enabling others to helm a team, head up a project, or serve as lead contact. Not only does this develop leadership capacity — which is necessary to growth — it is an act of liberation for the manager. Now she can sit back and do what good managers need to do — think and reflect. Too much of our management is putting out fires. So why not let others pour on the water while you watch their responsiveness and decisiveness. Better yet, think of ways to prevent fires from breaking out in the first place. That is, give yourself time to evaluate past actions, consider alternatives, and plan ahead in terms of processes and people. It is a win-win for both employees and managers who lead up.

Know That Time May Not Be on Your Side

To be honest, not all middle managers have the luxury of developing next generation leaders. Executives who specialize in turning around floundering companies are like smoke jumpers; the fire is raging nearly out of control, and it's their job to put out the flames and see what property can be saved or salvaged. Therefore, they must act first and listen later. But even then it is wholly appropriate to begin to lay the groundwork for how to get the enterprise running once it stops burning. Employees appreciate someone willing to jump into the breach, especially when it means saving their jobs.

Management is not a wholly hands-off activity. Like actor-directors, managers must sometimes step on stage and deliver their lines. One CEO of a publishing house has been known to pitch in with mailings during peak ordering seasons. Such examples are common in small- to medium-size businesses, but even in large enterprises, managers do the grunt work during times of crisis. For example, if a company is not performing up to par with its customers, senior leaders will fan out throughout the organization looking for answers everywhere from the factory floor to the top floor. Often such exercises end up educating the managers as much as they do alleviating customer problems. Middle managers learn more about the nuts and bolts of the business than from perches on mahogany row.

Too much direct engagement may have negative consequences. A manager must be an enabler. If she is doing the work of a subordinate, she is not enabling him to do his work. She is hindering his development as well as the development of the team. What's more, this extra work prevents her from thinking as a leader, one who is looking up at where the organization is going and how to bring people along. Too much micro-management, no matter how well intentioned, is costly in terms of wasted time and effort, not to mention thwarted career and personal development.

Management is often a thankless job, but getting off on the right foot is essential to all concerned. When a manager demonstrates a willingness to listen, he establishes himself as someone who cares about more than the work, but also about the people who do the work. There is a time for discipline and resolve, but it is often best to exert it along with care and concern for individuals.

Pulling for the team and standing aside for others to succeed works much of the time, but the leader needs to exert herself in tough times. This is a lesson that Dwight Eisenhower learned in North Africa when he became the first Allied commander supervising American, British, and French troops to oust the Axis powers from Morocco and Tunisia in 1942–1943. By nature, Ike was a genial, accommodating Kansan who drew people to him by the power of his intellect, his ability to plan, and his radiant personality. As Rick Atkinson tells it in his brilliant history, *An Army at Dawn*, those skills were put to the test, or more accurately, stressed to the breaking point, when the Allies — in particular, the Americans new to battle — suffered humiliating defeats against the German army and the numerous slights of British generals who thought him not up to the task. Ike held firm. In short, he learned to lead by finding the right people to lead the troops but at the same time balancing inconsistent political agendas from Washington, London, and Free France. Ike emerged from North Africa a better general, a better man, and the only one who could lead our Allies into Europe in the tough years ahead. It was a long way from Kansas, but Ike rose to the challenge and exerted leadership over his sometimes bickering team.[12]

When it comes to pulling together for a single goal, the sport of NASCAR serves as a good example. It is popular because it is fan friendly; there are cameras in the cars to enable people to see what drivers see. What's more, drivers at the track are like baseball players of three generations ago — ready, willing, and able to sign autographs and talk to the faithful. Why? Because drivers, together with their sponsors, realize that the sport, like all businesses, depends upon the support of paying customers. Leaders who succeed in business are those who focus their attention on customers and bring their people to the same point of view. The same holds for nonprofit entities — volunteers must be attuned to the needs of those they serve. It is the example of the leader that reminds them of this on a daily basis.

Leadership is not a solo act. It calls for an ability to stand tall on principle and values, but the ultimate measure of a leader is not principle per se, it is value-based results. Genuine leaders achieve them by tapping into the minds of their followers, and in the process, touching their hearts. Not for personal gain, but for the gain of the organizations, something that those who lead from the middle practice regularly. When leader and follower succeed together, everyone wins.

Putting people into positions where they can succeed is critical to organizational success as well as your own success. As we said at the outset of this chapter, your upward career path will be affected by how well you identify and nurture talent as well as your ability to get the most out of them. That, after all, is a key measurement of effective leadership. That will be an essential in how senior leaders will evaluate your readiness to move up in the organization.

What You Need to Do to Prepare Others to Lead

You need to be aware of those around you. No leader lives in a vacuum. It is imperative that you show people what you think of them. Honestly and positively. This means you coach your people for success. You communicate, cajole, and challenge. You also provide feedback. You make failure an option, not because you seek it, but because you know it is vital that people take risks before they can succeed.

To prepare others to lead, you will need to:

- Differentiate talent from skill.
- Make your leadership personal.
- Recognize achievement.
- Link better management to better leadership.
- Invest yourself in developing others.

LEADING WITH PRESENCE

Kindness in words creates confidence, kindness in thinking creates profoundness, kindness in giving creates love.

LAO-TZU[1]

■

It is said that you can judge the measure of a person by what people say after he passes. Well, if that's the case, then a football coach who passed away recently was revered. A press conference was held at the hospital in which he was taken after suffering a cardiac arrest, and in attendance were the university president, athletic director, and chief of cardiac care — all of whom drove 50 minutes on a moment's notice to pay an impromptu tribute to a man who had improved the lives of so many athletes, students, and ordinary people. He was Bo Schembechler, long-time coach of the University of Michigan football team, which he had led to 194 victories in a twenty-one-year span, never once experiencing a losing season.

Local media and national sports media devoted hours of coverage to mark his death, coming as it did on the eve of one of the biggest games in Michigan football history, playing archrival Ohio State. The teams were ranked numbers two and one respectively. Bo's legacy is not measured in terms of wins and losses, although those marks are considerable. What matters most to those who knew him as well as those who knew of him was his humanity, his ability to connect with his players, his coaches, and the community in ways that were visible on the field, but so especially evident in the lives of those he touched. In this way, Bo is a case study for those who want to know what makes a leader tick. Let me count some ways.

- *Teaching.* Bo turned boys into men. That may be a cliché today, but with Bo it was a promise, and something he said to the mothers of boys he recruited. He also committed that they would get an education, and a good one. On the field, he could be merciless and ruthless in meting out verbal punishment or temporary banishment for lessons un-learned. But as brutal as he could be, he always led with heart, letting players know that what he demanded was good for the team.
- *Conviction.* Bo believed in doing things the right way. Or not at all. His football program was clean, and the men who played for him, for the most part, did it his way, or they were off the team. In collegiate athletics there are many, and more so today, who cut corners due to the pressure of win-ning or the lure of the bigger paydays. None of that ever mattered to Bo. Either you played it straight and by the rules, or you didn't play at all.
- *Humility.* As up front as Bo was, he did know his limita-tions. On the last interview before he died, he joked that he was a has-been, an old coach who was just happy to be hanging around. Nothing could be further from the truth, but he knew his limitations and was careful not to overstep his bounds with current coaches.
- *Sharing.* There is a story about one of Bo's players who much later in life became quite ill and was hospitalized. The man drifted in and out of consciousness, but when he

awakened, who was by his bedside but his old coach. And by then Bo himself was not in good health but that didn't matter. His player needed him and Bo was there. That story is only one of hundreds told by his former players, so many of whom testify how he was there to congratulate them in good times and offer a helping hand in tough times.

- *Humor.* Bo loved sports and good jokes. He also never took himself (off the gridiron, that is) too seriously. He liked golf, and he was known to indulge in some good-natured swearing when he hit a bad shot. But it was all in good fun and often in the company of men he had coached. Levity and lightness added to his humanity.

Those who knew him will itemize many more attributes, of course, but one thing that rings true to the day he died was his commitment to young people. "Never again will we know the likes of Bo Schembechler," said Mary Sue Coleman, president of the University of Michigan and who came to know him only very late in his life. "And while we are saddened and stunned by his death, we are also filled with the gratitude that comes with warm memories. As individuals and as a university community, we enjoyed the privilege of knowing Bo and benefiting from his irrepressible personality and loyalty. He made Michigan a better university."

After he retired as coach and athletic director, he maintained an office in the athletic complex named for him, Schembechler Hall. He was always proud of his connection to the university, but he was careful never ever to interfere, even criticize one of his successors. He kept his distance, but he kept his door open. And so, sixteen years after he had coached his last game, young student athletes, not simply football players, would come by for a visit. Sometimes Bo would go after them. While he wouldn't dare question a coach's decision, he would frequently interject himself into the lives of student athletes whom he thought needed a little direction setting, chiefly for academic reasons. Few of them ever complained, but many voiced their appreciation for Bo's concern and caring.

And on the night before he died, he spoke to the Michigan team who would the next day go to Columbus to play Ohio State. Little of what he said was revealed at the time, but it is said that there was not a dry eye in the house. But two days later, when Michigan took the field in Ohio Stadium, his words, but more realistically, his example, were crystal clear. Play the game as a team. It's the surest path to victory.[2]

What Bo Schembechler Teaches Us About Leading Up:

- Put people into positions where they can succeed.
- Demonstrate toughness but back it with genuine concern and a passion for excellence.
- Understand that your values live on in those that you lead.

■ ■ ■

Few men ever wore their conviction on their faces the way that Bo Schembechler did. There was very little subtlety; he loved football. More, he loved teaching it and seeing how his players responded to his teaching and felt the passion that he did for the game and, most important, for the team. It was always the team for Bo. That's why you played the game. Not for yourself alone, but for the team. Passion, like the attributes of energy and resilience discussed earlier, is essential to leading up because it is the genuinely caring about results and how to achieve them. Passion in leaders is rooted in a concern for people, specifically in mobilizing them for a greater purpose. Passion also gives leaders a sense of presence, which is something those in all levels of leadership need to master.

Develop Leadership Presence

Passion and enthusiasm combine in the leader to create a sense of presence. More specifically, *leadership presence*, which I define as "earned authority." Presence is the tangible essence of power that flows from an individual's ability to do a job — and more specifically and importantly, to enable others to do their jobs individually and collectively. Those who lead up definitely need presence; it is fundamental to their credibility as people who can achieve results. Presence is the tangible manifestation of a leader's ability to connect honestly and authentically with others, especially with those who outrank him.

Cultivating presence is a conscious act, with the accent on *act*. So much of what leaders do is persuade others of the virtues of their ideas, whether those ideas come from the individual, the team, or the entire organization. To persuade you need to put yourself into it — to sell the concept. That requires conviction, yes, but conviction so evident that others can see, taste, and feel it. Doing it day after day requires a commitment to acting the part.

Such acting is not dissembling; it is enabling. What leaders must do is give people a reason to believe in the vision, the mission, and strategies. Leaders who embrace those ideas as their own and communicate them in thought, word, and deed are actors on the stage of organizational effectiveness.

Put Presence to Work

You can define presence in many different ways, but within leadership one definition that works for me is the "radiance of commitment." If you have ever had the opportunity to spend time with people who volunteer in social service jobs, be it work in hospitals, clinics, or with disadvantaged children, you can discern their commitment; it is almost palpable. Their commitment radiates with their enthusiasm for what they do: alleviating suffering or helping those in need succeed. The sense of mission that comes from volunteerism is different from the way people feel in the workplace, but the commitment to others must be there.

Those seeking to lead up must communicate passion for the work in two ways: one, a passion for the work itself; and two, a passion for the people who do the work. I have seen this passion at work in all kinds of situations from boardrooms to locker rooms, and even on the factory floor. In nearly every instance, the passion starts with the manager; she gets people excited about what they do, be it develop a strategy or lay wire for a new conduit. This excitement is backed by the commitment the manager shows to her people. They know she cares about them and therefore they want to work with her. That is leadership presence in action. So consider:

Talk Up the Work

Entrepreneurs excel in this aspect of business-building. They are enamored with the process of getting their product or service to market. When you are around such people, you can feel the enthusiasm they have for their work. And if the idea is good enough, others are attracted by the business and join it. They, too, talk up the work and how it benefits their customers.

Recognize the Work of Others

You create passion the same way you lead — by example. When a manager opens a staff meeting with a "pat on the back" to those who have done a good job, she is sending a message that contributions matter. When people feel that their work is important, they feel more important. And in time they may even feel some passion for what they do.

Celebrate the Work

Life is short, as the cliché goes, so why not do something about it? Make work fun. One way to make it more enjoyable is to celebrate the process. Stage a celebrate work lunch every quarter. Challenge people to come to the event with the outcomes of what they have done. For example, a computer programmer can invite a customer whose job has been made more efficient (and easier) by what the IT team has done. Other folks may want to brag about process and quality improvements. The point is to take a few hours off to have lunch, swap stories, and celebrate what you do for a living.

Be Present for the Team

Presence can be the essential element that brings excitement to the work effort. Those managers in the middle can nurture the creative spark to generate excitement. In a passionate workplace, when someone voices an idea or suggestion, it is met with a chorus of equally enthusiastic employees. Not everyone agrees, not by a long shot! But everyone seems to be excited about what they do and what they can do to contribute. That's the *passionate* difference. It is something that can be developed and celebrated through leaders who take the time to communicate their own values and beliefs in ways that validate the work and the people who do it.

You can get a feel for how enthusiasm matters by watching amateur athletes in action. The way they watch every play, eyes intent on the action, is a form of focused concentration. Similarly, when something goes well, they jump up and down as well as all over one another in an exhibition of exuberance. And when things turn sour, you see players put their arms around a player who's made a mistake, or players come together as a unit to listen to what the coach has to say in the final minutes. Enthusiasm can be the pick-me-up a team losing steam needs, or it can be the ingredient that puts a team on top into the cruising speed.

Enthusiasm is integral to the human condition and as such needs to find expression in the workplace. Successful sales teams live on enthusiasm; they live on the adrenaline that emerges from competition as well as the satisfaction that comes from meeting a sales goal. Similarly, engineers become enthused when a process they have been laboring over for months finally kicks into gear and works. Enthusiasm, as discussed in Step 1, is a healthy contagion, and one that managers leading up are wise to stoke. For example:

ADDRESS ATTITUDE

Much as enthusiasm is a collective emotion — that is, it reflects the outlook of the team — enthusiasm is part of the motivational process. Motivation is intrinsic; it bubbles within us. In his new book, *The Difference Maker*, leadership author John Maxwell identifies "five big obstacles: change, discouragement, failure, fear, and problems in general." Will you be overwhelmed, or will you overcome? "Your attitude is your choice," writes Maxwell.[3] That choice is personal, yes, but managers need to create conditions for people where people feel a part of team, and as such, feel their contributions matter. One way managers can demonstrate this is to talk about how much everyone on the team depends upon the work of others. That is an aspect of team that is often overlooked; others rely on their teammates, not simply to show up, but to produce. The manager who talks this up reminds others of their responsibility to team members.

Focus on the Team

Individuals matter, but within an organization, it's the collective output that counts. That's why we evaluate managers on what their team accomplishes, not necessarily what they promise the team will produce. Results are measured, and so too are managers. That's why the manager has to connect with people on the team to channel their energies toward team goals. Sometimes that focus is easy, like falling off a log; other times, particularly when times are tough, it may seem like climbing a mountain. That's where enthusiasm matters. It can provide the energy boost that teams need to survive, and ultimately thrive.

Look for Challenges

Teams that achieve are teams that are pushed, sometimes to the edge. The early days of our space program, in the 1960s, are a prime example. NASA collected some of the finest knowledge workers (and adventurers, too) in the world, gave them generous funding, and provided them with a sequence of never-ending challenges, putting men farther and farther into space until they reached the moon. The spirit among mission planners as well as engineers and astronauts was strong, even when beset by tragedies such as the fire that destroyed Apollo 1 and killed its astronauts. The big challenge of reaching the moon before the Soviets was in actuality the sum of the many challenges that each person at NASA felt in his job. For that reason, managers need to find the next hill to climb, be it developing a new product, reducing another defect, improving a process, or landing new customers. All are challenges that fuel enthusiasm.

Can you have too much enthusiasm? Of course. Times of crisis are not times for outward displays of enthusiasm. For example, if a new product bombs at launch or customers cease to buy your services, then that's a problem. It's nothing to celebrate. Better to focus that raw energy toward problem solving and eventual problem resolution than in back-slapping. What's more, such displays would make people suspicious; it would indicate that either the manager or the team was clueless about the magnitude of the crisis. At the same time, you want to generate enthusiasm about your ability to do your job. That's a necessary aspect of confidence, an emotion that very often accompanies enthusiasm.

Understand the Need for Optimism

Underlying enthusiasm is another emotion that is essential to leadership presence: optimism. If you have enough of it, you can accomplish great things, perhaps even get elected president. A team of research psychologists from the University of Pennsylvania have concluded that on the basis of a more than twenty-year research project into the topic. By analyzing stump speeches from presidential candidates since 1900, the researchers found that optimists trump pessimists more than 80 percent of the time. Why do optimists win? Martin Seligman, a member of the research team, told Bernard Carey of the *New York Times* that "We know that optimists tend to try harder under adversity, and that is a very important quality."[4] The 2008 election was a case in point. With the economy in decline, the candidate who radiated a greater sense of optimism, Barack Obama, trumped the candidate who seemed less comfortable with it, John McCain.

Optimism is essential to leadership. One reason is that leadership by nature is aspirational. It appeals to people to look up rather than down, to look at possibilities rather than obstacles, and to see opportunities where others see defeat. Optimism is rooted in hope. It provides people with a reason to believe in something better, that all things are possible. Certainly Ronald Reagan played this sentiment all the way to the White House in 1980. The country was in a muddle with rising inflation, a weak economy, and hostages trapped in a foreign embassy. Reagan recalled more prosperous times and rekindled the sense of American "can-doism." It was always there, of course; Reagan simply echoed it.

It is not simply presidents who need to look at the sunny side; all leaders must do so. Positivism is something that executive coaches counsel high potential leaders to radiate. Why? Because perpetual glumness is a downer; no one wants to follow a sour puss, let alone a committed pessimist. So what can you do to foster more optimism?

THINK OF POSSIBILITIES

Optimism is rooted in the art of making things happen. When problems occur, think first of ways to overcome them. Then look deeper to ways to capitalize on them. Entrepreneurs are noted for never knowing when to take no for an answer. They are preternaturally optimistic because they see opportunities where others see failure. They see brightness where others see darkness.

WELCOME NEW IDEAS

Optimists are people persons. They like meeting and mingling and sharing ideas. Good ideas are essential to finding new ways of doing things. By themselves ideas are cheap; good ideas translated into processes that save time and money and improve efficiency are the lifeblood of good companies. It takes an optimist to push ideas into action, especially when those ideas are not your own.

BE REALISTIC ABOUT OBSTACLES

Looking up, as optimists do, can cause you to run off the road, or even into walls. Too much optimism is like putting sugar on sugar-coated cereal or adding salt to potato chips. It's an overdose. Rationality, the ability to apply a cold, clinical eye to the situation, is essential. Otherwise, you will never accomplish anything and your happy talk will be just that. Talk!

Can you ever be too optimistic? Yes, just ask Michael Dukakis. The University of Pennsylvania's research team picked him to beat George H. W. Bush in 1988. Too much optimism is perceived as naiveté. People want their leaders to have a firm grasp of the situation and to be realistic about problems as well as possibilities. One who smiles at problems rather than tackling them is perceived as a lightweight. President Obama shifted his tone upon taking office. Elected as the optimistic candidate, with the economy in meltdown phase, he assumed a more realistic tone, putting the nation on notice that tough times lay ahead. Part of this was salesmanship for his economic stimulus package but also to be honest with the American people.[5]

See the Possibilities

A leader who looks at problems and sees possibilities for positive change is one whom people can follow. We want leaders to mobilize people to make a meaningful difference, even when it means making tough choices. But throughout tough times we want to follow someone who understands the severity but can still manage to be optimistic.[6] This presents good possibilities for leaders in the middle because they are in touch with the reality on the ground and can use that understanding to advocate more effectively.

While leadership presence may not be an absolute necessity, to my way of thinking, most leaders display it one way or another. It may be the way they engage others in conversation, acknowledge the contributions of others, or maintain their cool when everything and everyone around them are falling to pieces. It is not so much *what* these leaders do, it is *how* they do. With a combination of strength, purpose, and grace.

Leaders with presence are people we want to follow. Those are the leaders who have the trust of others. They do not blanch in the face of adversity. They know themselves inside and out. They can influence. They know how to develop others and put them into positions where they can succeed. They are leaders who can lead up and are ready for greater levels of responsibility, including one day leading the entire organization.

What You Need to Do to Lead with Presence

You need to lead yourself before you can lead others. You need to know what you are made up of. Character and conviction matter. You must also act the role of a leader by being present and available. Leaders set the right example. In truth, example is what counts most. It creates the foundation upon which trust can flourish. Your example is your character in action. Words matter sometimes; actions matter more.

To lead with presence, you will need to:

- Give people a reason to believe in you.
- Radiate confidence as well as optimism.
- Exude calmness in the face of adversity.
- Demonstrate passion and commitment for the work.
- Show appreciation for the work of others.
- Teach others by setting the example for emerging leaders to follow.

THE SMART GUIDE TO
POSITIVE PUSH-BACK

■

The premise of this book is that leading your boss is essential to helping your organization succeed. Toward that end, it is essential that you take responsibility for your own actions and in some cases exert that responsibility upward so that you can help the boss lead more effectively. Reality dictates, and this book demonstrates, that not all bosses want to be led. Some honestly fear that their authority is undermined. Others are so insecure that leadership from below is a threat that must be stamped out at all cost. If not, the boss could lose his or her job. Again, that's a real possibility. Such obstacles should not prevent an individual from seeking to lead his boss when appropriate. Consider the following information.

■ ■ ■

Stick with the Facts

Management is rooted in the validity of data. As leaders in the middle, it is essential that you build an argument to your boss that is based on valid data points. And here's what you can do to ensure that you are building your arguments with facts that are valid as well as on point.

- *Keep digging.* Given the fact that we want proof for our own ideas, we need to have the courage to see if data can be found for other points of view. Investigative reporters do this routinely when seeking to corroborate their stories. They look for people who can back up the story as well as those who can dispute facts. The more they dig, the more they uncover points that either support or disprove the story line.

- *Ask people to challenge the premise.* When major decisions are under review, it is wise to ask trusted associates to play the role of devil's advocate. Challenge them to challenge your assumptions. Such thinking will do one of two things: one, disprove your premise and cause you to rethink a course of action; or two, validate your assumptions and give you more confidence in your ultimate decision.

- *Do not confuse causation with correlation.* Put simply, just because there is a link between two issues does not mean one provoked the other. For example, let's say the market rises on four consecutive Tuesdays. Is there a correlation between the second day of the business week and an increase in stock prices? Yes. Does Tuesday cause the market to rise? No. Correlation therefore does not imply causation, yet we often equate the two. This is one reason among many that consumer research can point marketers in wrong directions if studies are not conducted properly.

Of course, there may be a pitfall in pushing for more and more data. It's called stalling, or what many refer to as "analysis paralysis." That tactic is nothing more than a decision-avoidance mechanism. When managers do not want to decide, they ask for more and more data. Sooner or later data will contradict itself; that throws even more confusion on the process, but it will get the manager off the hook and forestall decisions. That is, collect what you need and then structure your argument.

Deal with the Jerk

Sometimes all the good data will not convince your boss that you are right. Sometimes the clarity of your argument reveals the character of the "jerk boss." Truly jerk bosses are those that are typically insecure; they vent and act tough because inside they are afraid of losing their jobs. They seek to dominate rather than cooperate because it gives them a sense of control. Such bosses are not rational; that is, they cannot be reasoned with. So do not try. There are three things you can do: roll over, fight back, or leave. Let's take them one at a time.

1. *If you want to keep your job, go with the flow and avoid confrontation.* Do not provoke your boss; always keep civil even when he is not. Prepare for the worst, but keep your head about you.

2. *If on the other hand, you are tired of being pushed around, and your teammates feel the same, then devise strategies to circumvent your boss.* Take the high road. Do your work the best you can. Document things the boss does incorrectly, such as managing tasks, dealing with subordinates, offering proper supervision, and maintaining control. Do not focus on attitude; document behavior. Also, note the effect the boss is having on the team with regards to productivity, absenteeism, turnover, and relations with other teams. Again, document. When you've gathered your evidence, present it to someone in authority. [*Work closely with a trusted associate in human resources.*] Be very careful. Many times jerk bosses have friends in high places who will not appreciate having their people criticized. You could lose your job. Understand that.

3. *If things get too bad, then you have only one real option.* Leave! Look to transfer to another department. If that is not feasible, then consider opportunities at other organizations. Plan carefully.

Bounce Back

All of us have moments when things do not go our way. Setbacks are nothing new and will always be with us. What matters is how we recover. The essence of a good comeback is resilience. My personal metaphor for resilience is the sapling. Plant it in the fall, then watch it bend, sometimes to the ground, in strong winter winds. Come spring, it straightens back up, reaching for the light. And it grows taller and wider until, in future years, it is a mature tree whose branches rustle but whose trunks stand firm and proud even in the fiercest winds. When your next setback occurs, here are some questions to consider:

- *What happened?* Analyze the situation. What went wrong and why? Consider the facts as well as your actions. Ask others for their perspective. Their point of view is more objective than yours. Listen to what they say.
- *What could I have done better?* Once you have the facts, think about what you could have done to overcome the obstacles. Perhaps you could have done a better job of anticipating disaster. Or should you have taken immediate steps rather than holding back and waiting? As you sift through the situation objectively as possible (and yes, it's hard), think of alternate courses of action.
- *What did I learn?* Most important, stand back and reflect. What did this setback teach you? Perhaps it means you will need to rely on your people more. Or you will need to gain more skills prior to tackling this kind of assignment. Whatever you decide, learn from it and prepare for the next time. Bottom line, if you have not learned anything, then you are back to square one.

Resilience is the steel in the spine of the leader who leads his or her boss and colleagues. Resilience gives you the strength you need even in the toughest of times. What distinguishes those who succeed is bouncing back from that raw deal so that they remain focused on their goals and engaged in the process of fulfilling them. Doing that is the measure of a determined and successful leader.

NOTES

■

Prologue

1. *FastCompany's The rules of business* (New York: Doubleday, 2005), p. 99.
2. Michael Useem, *Leading up: How to lead your boss so you both win* (New York: Crown, 2001), p. 6.
3. Truman and Emerson quotes from www.coolquotes.com
4. Watson Wyatt Worldwide from Nic Patton, "Fewer than half of U.S. Workers trust their boss." Retrieved from www.ManagementIssues.com 01/05/07
5. Nic Patton, "CEOs starting to run out of answers," *Management-Issues.com* (January 23, 2009), citing Booz & Company December 2008 survey of 800+ senior managers ("Recession response: Why companies are making the wrong moves." Research by Shumeet Banjeri, Neil McArthur, Cesare Mainardi, Carlos Ammann www.booz.com)
6. Nic Patton, "CEOs worried by new generation of managers," www.management-issues.com (October 5, 2007), citing Conference Board study; Nic Patton, "U.S. suffering a critical shortage of middle managers," www.management-issues.com (May 17, 2007), citing Bersin & Associates study.
7. VitalSmarts/Concours Group, "Silence fails: The five crucial conversations for flawless execution," *Management Issues News* (October 11, 2006).
8. "Managers critical to employee engagement," *www.management-issues.com* (November 9, 2006), citing Doug Jensen, Tom McMullen, Mel Stark, *The Manager's Guide to Rewards* (New York: AMACOM, 2006).
9. Kelly School of Business, Indiana University. (2006). The Indiana study correlates to research conducted by Dr. Mitch Neubert and H. R. Gibson, Chair of Management Development at Hankamer School of Business (Baylor University) and C. Longnecker. N = 830 managers/166 focus groups. Research was included in Mitch Neubert and Clinton Longnecker, "Why managers fail to get results in rapidly changing organizations: Causes, consequences and cures," *Baylor Business Review* (Fall 2004).

Step 1

1. Robert A. Fitton, Compiler, *Leadership: Quotes from the world's greatest motivators* (Boulder, CO: Westview Press/Harper Collins, 1997), p. 47.
2. This biographical sketch draws most heavily on Doris Kearns Goodwin, *No ordinary time* (New York: Simon & Schuster, 1993). Other sources include Jonathan Alter, *The defining moment* (New York: Simon & Schuster, 2007); Interview with H.W. Brands, author of *Traitor to his class: The privileged life and radical presidency of Franklin Delano Roosevelt* (New York: Doubleday, 2008), *Diane Rehm Show* NPR December 26, 2008.
3. Excerpt from Eleanor Roosevelt's speech on the Universal Declaration of Human Rights, http://www.udhr.org/history/frbioer.htm
4. A portion of this chapter first appeared as a column ("Great leaders build great relationships") in CIO.com November 2007.

Step 2

1. Robert A. Fitton, Compiler, *Leadership: Quotes from the world's greatest motivators* (Boulder, CO: Westview Press/Harper Collins, 1997), p. 272.
2. Bio sketch was drawn from Frank Deford, "Edmund Hillary, the humble conqueror," *Morning Edition* (January 16, 2008); Robert McFadden, "Edmund Hillary, first on Everest, dies at 88," *New York Times* (January 11, 2008); "Plain man, mighty deeds," *Economist* (January 19, 2008).
3. Edward deBono, *Lateral thinking* (New York: Harper Paperbacks, 1973); Edward deBono, *Six thinkinats*, 2nd ed. (Boston: Little, Brown/Back Bay Books, 1999). See also www.edwdebono.com
4. Don Altman, *Living kindness* (Makawao, Maui, HI: Inner Ocean Publishing, 2003), p. 53.
5. Bill Joy, "Large problem: How big companies can innovate," *Fortune* (November 15, 2004).
6. Douglas Brinkley, *Wheels for the world and a century of progress, 1903–2003* (New York: Viking Books, 2003).
7. Gautam Naik, "A hospital races to learn of Ferrari pit stop," *Wall Street Journal* (November 14, 2006).
8. A portion of this chapter referencing benchmarking first appeared as a column ("Beyond benchmarking") for CIO.com (September 12, 2007). Used with permission.

9. Mihaly Csikszentmihalyi, *Flow: The psychology of optimal experience* (New York: Harper Perennial, 1991).

10. Johan Jorgensen, "How to pump out profits for over 100 Years," *Business 2.0* (August 2004).

11. Allen Barra, *The last coach* (New York: W.W. Norton & Co., 2005), p. 258.

12. Ibid., citing *The legend of Bear Bryant* by Mickey Herskowitz.

13. Gregory L. White, "A mismanaged palladium stockpile was catalyst for Ford's write-off." *Wall Street Journal* (February 6, 2002).

14. The author would like to thank David Soubly, IT professional and author, for assistance with this section of the chapter on knowledge networks.

Step 3

1. Robert A. Fitton, *Leadership: Quotes from the world's greatest motivators* (Boulder, CO: Westview Press/Harper Collins, 1997), p. 151.

2. Holly Cain, "In the fast lane: Newman racing career no act," *Seattle Post-Intelligencer* (October 2, 2008); Bill Dwyre, "Racing loses a cool hand in Paul Newman," *Los Angeles Times* (September 28, 2008).

3. "Tribute to Paul Newman," *Larry King Live* CNN, September 27, 2008.

4. "Newman's legacy: Good works," *Associated Press* (CNN.com) (September 29, 2008).

5. Except where noted, all facts and quotes are derived from Aljean Harmetz, "Paul Newman, a magnetic titan of Hollywood, is dead at 83," *New York Times* (September 28, 2008).

6. John Baldoni, *Great communication secrets of great leaders* (New York: McGraw Hill, 2003), pp. 121–124; Thomas J. Neff and James M. Citrin, *Lessons from the top: The search for America's best business leaders* (New York: Currency/Doubleday, 1999), pp. 345–346.

7. Rich Teerlink and Lee Ozley, *More than a motorcycle: The leadership journey at Harley-Davidson* (Boston: Harvard Business School Press, 2000) pp. 197–198.

8. Renee Montagne, "U.S. preps new embassy in Baghdad" [Interview with Ambassador Frank Ricciardone], *Morning Edition*, National Public Radio (June 23, 2004).

9. Ed Cray, *General of the Army: George C. Marshall, soldier statesman* (New York: Cooper Square Press, 2000).

10. Victor Davis Hanson, *Soul of battle: From ancient times to the present day, how three great liberators vanquished tyranny* (New York: Anchor Books/Doubleday, 2001).

11. Chris Matthews, *Hardball* (New York: Touchstone Press, 1988, 1999), pp. 133–135.

12. Eric Hoffer quote is from creatingminds.org. Jan Carlzon is featured in many business case studies. His book, *Moments of truth* (New York: Collins Business 1989), is classic tome on customer service.

Step 4

1. Robert A. Fitton, Compiler. *Leadership: Quotes from the world's greatest motivators* (Boulder, CO: Westview Press/Harper Collins, 1997), p. 137.

2. Jim Collins, *Good to great* (New York: Harper Business, 2001), pp. 83–87.

3. James B. Stockdale, "Machiavelli, management, and moral leadership," in Malham M. Wakin and James Kempf (eds.), *Military ethics: Reflections on principles: Profession of arms, military leadership, ethical practices, war & morality, educating the citizen-soldier* (Washington, DC: National Defense University Press, 1987). [Originally published as Proceedings, U.S. Naval Institute, 1980.]

4. Joseph J. Ellis, *His Excellency: George Washington* (New York: Random House/Vintage, 2004, 2005), p. 139.

5. Jim Collins, *Good to great, op. cit.*

6. Anne Fisher, "Retain your brains," *Fortune* (July 24, 2006).

7. Mark Heller, "Ramsey 'a perfect fit,'" *Ann Arbor News* (March 13, 2005).

8. John Madden during game between the Patriots and Colts, *Monday Night Football*, ABC Sports (September 9, 2004).

9. Chris Matthews, *Hardball* (New York: Simon & Schuster/Touchstone, 1988, 1999), p. 69.

10. The author would like to acknowledge Michael Szwarcbord and Sue O'Neill of the Flinders Medical Centre for their presentation, "Redesigning care: Improving the patient journey," which was delivered at the University of Michigan Health System on July 5, 2006.

11. Malcolm Brown, *The imperial war museum: Book of the Somme* (London: Pan Books, 1997).

12. Watson Wyatt on communications; Towers Perrin, "Employee disengagement a global epidemic," www.ManagementIssues.com (November 16, 2005).

13. John F. Love, *Behind the arches: The story of McDonald's* (New York: Bantam, 1995).

Step 5

1. *FastCompany's The rules of business* (New York: Doubleday, 2005), p. 103.
2. Geraldine Sealey, "Bono on the barricades," *Salon.com* (May 17, 2004).
3. "Time 100: The lobbyist rock star," CNN.com (April 19, 2004).
4. Interview with Bill O'Reilly, *The O'Reilly Factor*, Fox News (September 1, 2004).
5. Ibid.
6. Ibid.
7. "Bono urges West to fight for Africa," Reuters (May 17, 2004).
8. Nancy Gibb, "The Good Samaritans," *Time* (December 10, 2005).
9. Geraldine Sealey, "Bono on the barricades," op. cit.
10. The author would like to note that this section, which includes the push/pull concept and various aspects of persuasion, was adapted from material and models developed by Dorthea Mahan, Ph.D, and Janice Krupic of Paragon Leadership, Inc. www.paragon-lead.com.
11. Fred Vogelstein, "Innovation entrepreneurs: It's not just business, it's personal: Eric Schmidt," *Fortune* November 11, 2004.
12. Kate Bonamici, "Innovation entrepreneurs: You do the dishes, I'll mind the store: Howard Lester," *Fortune* (November 15, 2004).
13. Christopher Tkaczyk, "Innovation entrepreneurs: The best ideas come from the front line: Scott Cook," *Fortune* (November 15, 2004).
14. Ron Winslow, "In line to lead: Dr. Susan Desmond-Holland," *Wall Street Journal* (November 19, 2004). [In 2009, Dr. Susan Desmond-Hellmann was named chancellor of the University of California, San Francisco.]
15. Masaaki Imai, *Gemba Kaizen* (New York: McGraw-Hill, 1997), pp. xxiv, 13, 14.
16. Michael Barbaro, "Wal-Mart chief makes plea to states on health care," *New York Times* February 27, 2006); Michael Barbaro, "Wal-Mart enlists bloggers in its public relations campaign," *New York Times* (March 7, 2006).
17. A portion of this chapter dealing with ingenuity first appeared in a column ("The case for advocacy") CIO.com June 2, 2006. Used with permission.

Step 6

1. Robert A. Fitton, Compiler, *Leadership: Quotes from the world's greatest motivators* (Boulder, CO: Westview Press/Harper Collins, 1997), p. 99.

2. *Rx for survival — The Heroes*, PBS, aired April 12, 2006; Global Health Champions, *Rx for survival — The Heroes*, www.pbs.org/wgbh/rxforsurvival. For more on the Bangladesh Rural Advancement Committee visit www.brac.net

3. *Clint Eastwood: Out of the Shadows*, Directed by Bruce Ricker and written by Dave Kehr (2000) for PBS American Masters series.

4. David Simon, *Homicide: A year on the killing streets* (New York: Ivy Books/Balantine Books, 1993).

5. Michael Useem, "Thinking like a guide," in *Upward Bound* (New York: Crown Business, 2003), p. 206.

6. Isaiah Berlin, "Mr. Churchill," *The Atlantic* (September 1949); Isaiah Berlin, "Churchill and Roosevelt," excerpt from Winston Churchill (1940) www.rjgeib.com/heroes/berlin/churchill-roosevelt.html

7. Rudy Tomjanovich story is from contemporaneous accounts of his resignation; John Feinstein, *The punch: One night, two lives, and the fight that changed basketball forever* (Boston: Little, Brown, 2002).

Step 7

1. Ted Goodman, Editor, *Forbes book of business quotations* (New York: Black Dog & Leventhal Publishers, 1997), p. 644.

2. This profile is compiled from a number of contemporary sources including Barack Obama's speeches as well as Ryan Lizza, "Making it: How Chicago shaped Obama," *The New Yorker* (July 21, 2008); Ryan Lizza, "Battle plans: How Obama won," *The New Yorker* (November 17, 2008); "The choice," Frontline, PBS 2008 (October 14, 2008); Chris Cilizza, *Hardball with Chris Matthews*, MSNBC (December 3, 2008).

3. Judy Battista, "Patriots' Brady on a comfort level, still ascending," *New York Times* (January 26, 2004).

4. Abraham Lustgarten, "Innovation entrepreneurs: A hot steaming cup of customer awareness: Howard Schultz," *Fortune* (November 15, 2004).

5. Interview with Jeff Garcia, Baltimore Ravens vs. Cleveland Browns, *ESPN Sunday Night Football* (November 7, 2004).

6. Abraham Lustgarten, *op. cit.*

7. Interview with Russell Simmons, *They made America*, Executive Producer Harold Evans, PBS, originally broadcast November 8, 2004.

8. Geoffrey C. Ward, *A first-class temperament* (New York: Harper & Row, 1989), pp. 84–94.

9. The author would like to thank Lt. Col. Chris Lucier USA (retired) for his insights into this essay on composure.

10. John Wooden with Steve Jamison, *Wooden* (New York: Contemporary Books, 1997).

11. Jim Collins, *Good to great and the social sectors: A monograph to accompany Good to Great* (New York Harper Collins, 2005). Adapted from a presentation delivered by Jim Collins at the Wharton Leadership Conference, June 13, 2006.

12. Jonah Keri, "Managing for success: It's not about your good ideas," *Investor's Business Daily* (November 8, 2004).

13. Bo Burlingame, "Coolest small company in America," *Inc* magazine (January 2003). Zingerman's was later featured in Bo Burlingame, *Small giants* (New York: Penguin/Portfolio Trade, updated edition 2007); quote from Paul Saginaw was from an interview with the author in 2004.

Step 8

1. *FastCompany's The rules of business* (New York: Doubleday, 2005), p. 101.

2. Interview by Tom Brokaw with David Gregory, *Meet the Press* NBC (transcript) (December 7, 2008). The MSNBC website, www.msnbc.com, contains biographical information and remembrances.

3. Profile of Beverly Sills was drawn from: Anthony Tommasini, "Beverly Sills, All-American diva, is dead at 78," *New York Times* (July 3, 2007); Mark Feeney, "Beverly Sills, people's diva, dies," *Boston Globe* (July 3, 2007); Manuela Hoelterhoff, "Sills-super diva, goofball, stock picker," *Bloomberg.com* (July 3, 2007).

4. Michael Mink, "Football Coach Paul 'Bear' Bryant," *Sports Leader & Success Investor's Business Daily* (New York: McGraw-Hill, 2004 [Originally published in IBD 10/23/00). Quotes are from Paul Bryant and John Underwood, *Bear* (Boston: Little, Brown, 2007).

5. Ibid., p. 22.

6. Marcus Buckingham and Curt Coffman, *First, break all the rules* (New York: Simon & Schuster, 1999).

7. Quote by John W. Gardner is from www.leadershipnow.com. For more insights, read John W. Gardner, *On leadership* (New York: Free Press, 1989).

8. John Baldoni, *Personal leadership, taking control of your work life* (Rochester, MI: Elsewhere Press, 2001).

9. Joyce Doria, Horacio Rozanski, and Ed Cohen, "What business needs from business schools," *Strategy + Business 32* (Fall 2003).

10. Warren G. Bennis, "The seven ages of the leader," *Harvard Business Review* (January 2004).

11. D. Michael Abrashoff, *It's your ship: Management techniques from the best damn ship in the Navy* (New York: Warner Business Books, 2002), pp. 159–160.

12. Rick Atkinson, *Army at dawn* (New York: Simon & Schuster, 2003).

Step 9

1. Ted Goodman, Editor, *Forbes book of business quotations* (New York: Black Dog & Leventhal Publishers, 1997), p. 469.

2. This account is drawn from contemporary accounts of Bo Schembechler's death that occurred in November 2006. Source material was drawn from Bo's memorial service held in Michigan Stadium on November 21, 2006, as well as newspapers such as the *Ann Arbor News*, *Detroit Free Press*, and the *Detroit News*. Also radio commentaries by John U. Bacon (co-author with Bo Schembechler) of *Bo's lasting lessons* (New York: Warner Books, 2007).

3. John C. Maxwell, *The difference maker* (Nashville, TN: Nelson Books, 2006); Paul B. Brown, "Attitude isn't everything, but it's close," *New York Times* (August 6, 2006).

4. Bernard Carey, "Handicapping with optimism," *New York Times* (May 1, 2007).

5. Based upon contemporaneous news reports including Anderson Cooper, *AC, 360*, CNN (February 20, 2009).

6. Bernard Carey, "Handicapping with optimism," *op. cit.*

INDEX

ABOUT THE AUTHOR

John Baldoni is an internationally recognized leadership consultant, speaker, and author of many books, including *Lead by Example: 50 Ways Great Leaders Inspire Results,* which received two "book of the month" mentions and a "best leadership book" for 2008. John writes the weekly "Leadership at Work" column for Harvard Business that is syndicated by Bloomberg.com. His leadership articles also have appeared in BusinessWeek.com, the Washington Post.com, and the WallStreetJournal.com. John has been featured or quoted in many publications, including the *New York Times, USA Today,* the *Chicago Tribune,* and *Investor's Business Daily.* Visit him at www.johnbaldoni.com.